Stopping Family Violence

ACKNOWLEDGMENTS

This report was sponsored by the Conrad N. Hilton Foundation of Los Angeles, California. I want to express special appreciation for both financial and moral support.

Individuals who challenge our collective assumptions about the field of family violence are all too rare. One such person was Terry W. McAdam, Executive Vice President of the Conrad N. Hilton Foundation. He spurred researchers, practitioners, policymakers, and activists to work together to clarify what knowledge was needed to end violence in families. This agenda's genesis was in Terry's desire for understanding what was known about the field, thereby enabling people to achieve their goals with purpose and to base their actions on solid evidence. He never intended this document to sit on the shelf; it is, rather, a call to action. Because Terry W. McAdam died before he could see the outcome of his efforts, this agenda is dedicated to him.

Stopping Family Violence

Research Priorities for the Coming Decade

DAVID FINKELHOR

with

Gerald T. Hotaling & Kersti Yllö

SAGE PUBLICATIONS
The Publishers of Professional Social Science
Newbury Park   Beverly Hills   London   New Delhi

For information address:

SAGE Publications, Inc.
2111 West Hillcrest Drive
Newbury Park, California 91320

SAGE Publications Inc.   SAGE Publications Ltd.
275 South Beverly Drive   28 Banner Street
Beverly Hills   London EC1Y 8QE
California 90212   England

SAGE PUBLICATIONS India Pvt. Ltd.
M-32 Market
Greater Kailash I
New Delhi 110 048 India

Printed in the United States of America

Library of Congress Cataloging-in-Publication Data

Finkelhor, David.
    Stopping family violence : research priorities for the coming
decade / by David Finkelhor with Gerald Hotaling and Kersti Yllö.
        p. cm.
    "A report sponsored by the Conrad N. Hilton Foundation, of Los Angeles,
California."
    Bibliography: p.
    ISBN 0-8039-3215-4 :
    1. Family violence—Research—United States.   2. Child abuse—
Research—United States.   3. Wife abuse—Research—United States.
I. Hotaling, Gerald T.   II. Yllö, Kersti.   III. Conrad N. Hilton
Foundation.   IV. Title.
HQ809.3.U5F56 1988
362.8′2—dc19   87-27972
                                                          CIP

FIRST PRINTING 1988

CONTENTS

ACKNOWLEDGMENT OF CONSULTANTS

Many different individuals served as consultants to this project, contributing their suggestions and reviewing and scoring priorities. Many of them are researchers prominent in the field of family violence. Some are in policy positions with national and governmental organizations. Some are practitioners and advocates for victims of family violence. We regard the participation of this latter group as particularly important, since cooperation between researchers and practitioners/ activists is so crucial to family violence research, and the relationship between these groups has had its difficult moments.

Most of the studies included here came from suggestions of one or several of the consultants to the agenda. However, we decided not to give specific credit for specific suggestions—both because the attribution of origination was unclear in many cases and also because many of the suggestions went through transformations that their originators would not necessarily have endorsed. But these consultants were an integral part of the process, and the agenda is meant to be a creative consensus of their suggestions and ideas. We are very indebted for their help.

David Adams, Chris Bagley, Judith Becker, Lucy Berliner, Bud Bolton, Angela Browne, Ann Burgess, Robert Burgess, Mary Capps, Ann Cohn, Anita Coll, Jon Conte, David Corwin, Deborah Daro, Jeffery Edelson, Michelle Fine, Loretta Fredericks, Irene Frieze, James Garbarino, Edward Gondolf, Richard Gelles, Robert Hampton, Ray Helfer, Judith Herman, Roy Herrenkohl, Sharon Herzberger, Nancy King, Richard Krugman, Joan Kuriansky, Donna LeClerc, Lisa Lerman, Judith Martin, Eli Newberger, Mildred Pagelow, Jim Ptacek, Ellen Pence, Robert Pierce, Robert Prentky, Vernon Quinsey, Carl Rogers, Desmond Runyan, Diana Russell, Daniel Saunders, Susan Schechter, Nancy Shields, Murray Straus, Lenore Walker, David Wolfe.

We want to particularly thank Barbara Hart and the Institute for Women's Leadership for their initiative in recruiting suggestions from a wide network of people and for contributing to the section on ethical issues.

1

INTRODUCTION

In recent years, concern over the problem of family violence has inspired many journal articles, prompted much legislation, and catalyzed the development of new agencies and social programs. But after a generation of frenetic social activity to combat family violence, the signs of progress are uncertain. If we simply count programs or publications or services provided, the results look impressive. But if we ask how often family violence has been halted, how much it has decreased, and how many of its negative effects have been mitigated, the answer is unknown. Part of the problem in combating family violence lies in the difficulty of the task. The family is among the most basic, complex, and intense of all human institutions. Within it, we are trying to tame two of the most primal and unruly of all human impulses—aggression and sex. No wonder some regard the task as doomed to failure. But more of the problem lies with limitations of our own knowledge. We do not fully understand the sources of family violence. We do not know precisely what to do to stop it. And we have made only a limited effort to evaluate the effectiveness of what we already have done. The irony is, we may have actually made giant strides toward ameliorating the problem, and simply may not know it.

However, the uncertainty of our efforts so far should not be cause for pessimism. While the difficulties of the task are not within our power to change, the limits of our knowledge are. There is increasingly wide consensus among policymakers and practitioners that we could be much more optimistic about the problem of family violence if we had more and better research into its causes and effects, and our efforts to deal with them.

The goal of this book is to foster more and better research into the problem of family violence. It intends to contribute to that goal in a number of concrete ways.

First, this book will try to focus opinion in the field on what needs to be done. There are a vast number of research questions that might be undertaken. But some may have already been answered, others may have little hope of being answered, and still others may be very marginal in their usefulness. The proposals for research presented here have been chosen for their urgency to the field. In the descriptions of each, we have explained why they are so important. The answers they would provide would have an impact on the largest number of people in the largest domains of social policy and practice.

A second important goal of this report is to attract new researchers into the field. Family violence is still not well studied, in part because not enough researchers are interested in it. Why researchers decide to study one problem and not another is a complicated matter. But to some extent researchers are more likely to be attracted to a field in which they see interesting and researchable questions to address and an opportunity to make an important contribution. To the extent that this report outlines the interesting questions and shows the utility of their answers, it should help to attract new researchers.

Another goal of this book is to attract and orient new funding sources. Until now, funds for family violence research have mostly come from the federal government. In part, this reflects the infancy of the research tradition in this field, which has not yet developed a broad constituency in the public and private sectors. But there is every reason to believe that family violence research can interest a broader range of funding sources. It is a serious social problem, one which generates substantial concern at both the public and the professional level. The opportunity for social and public policy impact is significant. What may be needed to interest some of these potential funding sources is simply (1) to be shown detailed plans for research projects that have been carefully thought out and about which there is some consensus, and (2) to be convinced that this research will have some major policy payoffs. This book is dedicated to developing those kinds of research plans and illustrating their payoff.

In addition to potential funders, there are other public and private policymakers who need to be oriented to the field of family violence research. Some of these people make decisions about research funding and others about practice and service provision. They will be crucial players in any major research undertaking. For them to be thinking about and prepared for a major research agenda in the field of family violence makes it all the more likely that such research will happen. This book is intended to help them develop their thoughts about the research to come. Finally, this book is intended as a kind of benchmark. It is a statement of where the field is in 1988—what has been done and what still needs to be done in the minds of people very active in the field. It will be a document that can be reviewed in 5 or 10 years to see how much progress we have made, how perceptions have changed, and how much has been accomplished. It is hoped that we will be pleased by the results.

Approach to This Project

The plans for this book emerged out of conversations between a proactive charitable foundation with continuing interest in the field of family violence and a research center with a lengthy history of contributions to the same. The goals were to reach all the various audiences just described with a document describing the highest priority research projects needed in the field. The intention of the document was to reflect the thinking of the field as a whole, not simply one or several individuals. With that in mind, it was decided to draw on the ideas of a wide variety of people. A list was drawn up, consisting of researchers, practitioners, activists, and policymakers who had been active in the field for some time and had had some previous opportunity to think about research priorities. Given time constraints, the list of people consulted was far from comprehensive. It was organized to include representatives from a variety of domains and perspectives, and some who could propose priorities in specific areas. Because it dealt with research, researchers were clearly overrepresented on the list. Altogether over four dozen individuals were contacted. Each respondent was asked to think about and respond to nine questions. The questions were designed to evoke a broad perspective and to jar respondents from their own narrow area of specialization to consider the field as a whole. The questions presumed that research priorities would differ depending on goals. So respondents were asked to think of research projects that would be of importance to such diverse goals as prevention, intervention, advancing public interest in the problem, and solving some important problems of research methodology. The questions were as follows:

(1) What do you see as our most obvious gap in knowledge and what research project(s) would best fill that gap?
(2) Given unlimited resources, what is the study you would most like to see done?
(3) What is the social policy question in the field that most urgently needs an answer? What study would you propose to answer that question?

(4) Can you think of more field experiments (like Sherman and Berk's study of arresting wife batterers) that badly need to be done? What would be the most important one and how would you go about it?

(5) If you had $500,000 to conduct a research study that would bear results in *preventing* this type of family violence, what would it be?

(6) If you had $500,000 to conduct a research study that would bear results on the *detection of victims or offenders,* what would it be?

(7) If you had $500,000 to conduct a research study that would bear results on *how to intervene or how to treat victims or offenders,* what would it be?

(8) What is an example of a research study you would propose to most immediately advance and develop methodology in this field?

(9) What is the research study you would propose to most immediately mobilize public and governmental support for greater attention to the problem of family violence and abuse?

(10) What is the next study that you yourself are planning to do, if you are a researcher?

In response to these questions, we received dozens of suggestions. There was considerable overlap but there was also a great diversity. When it was clear that certain suggestions were appearing again and again, we made particular note of this, and tried to get respondents to be more specific, to set out just how they thought this project should be done. We called some respondents back and confronted them with the ideas of others to see if they would agree or disagree. Then we took all the suggestions we had received, brought them together with our own criteria of what constituted a priority, and distilled a draft of this document. To give respondents one more opportunity to have an input, we distributed drafts of the priorities to most of the original respondents and asked for their further comments. We also asked them to rank the priorities in their order of importance. The outcome of this process resulted in the priorities listed here. Their ordering reflects the ranking respondents gave them.

One observation we made about this process was telling. We believed we had selected questions that would encourage people to think big. In several, respondents were told to disregard costs and in others given the figure of $500,000, a healthy-sized budget for a research project. This was so people would think in terms of what needed to be done, not just what was feasible or would be supported under current funding arrangements.

Even with these encouragements, however, we weren't always successful. We were disappointed to note that, apparently as a result of a long era in which support for social science research has been quite limited, researchers and policymakers seem to think instinctively in modest terms. Many have never even considered whether a large-scale and powerful social experiment could provide the answers. Many dismissed such ideas as politically unfeasible, even if they might work scientifically. For our part, however, we have not in this document tried to scale projects down to acceptable conventional budgetary constraints. We have presented proposals of studies that needed to be done whatever the cost. Perhaps if the notion of large-scale experiments was revived and seriously discussed, it could eventually gain support in political circles.

Topics Covered

In name, this book is concerned with family violence. In reality, it is about three particular family problems: physical child abuse, sexual child abuse, and spouse abuse. All three fall under the rubric of family violence, but other things do as well, including violence between siblings and violence against elderly family members. Unfortunately, *family violence* does not have a commonly accepted definition and a commonly accepted set of components. It is a term that has been defined by social movements and used in different ways at different times.

Our decision to limit this book to child abuse, sexual abuse, and spouse abuse is based on practical rather than philosophical considerations. These are three areas within the field of family violence that are regarded as in very urgent need of attention based on prior research into their scope and effects. They are also areas that are of concern to a wide array of practitioners and policymakers. Given limited time and limited resources, we judged it preferable to focus attention to these three rather than spread our efforts more thinly over the entire field.

Assumptions Behind This Book

Several assumptions lie behind all the research priorities outlined here, and it would do well to mention them at the beginning. The first, and perhaps most obvious, is that research into these problems is important and makes a major contribution to their solution. Stated this way, such an assertion sounds like a platitude. But in practical terms, its implications are controversial because the need for research is often neglected even by those who support it in principle. It is easy to understand why. Family violence is a poignant and distressing problem with very real victims who need immediate attention. There is almost no one in this field who disagrees with the idea that attention to victims should occupy the first priority. However, the urgency of the plight of victims in a world of scarce resources does not relent and thus poses a continuing dilemma. Is it ethical to spend scare resources on research when there appears to be less than enough to deal with the immediate suffering of victims? Although few people disagree with the importance of research in the abstract, when faced with this concrete trade-off between research and services, there are some who would allocate little or nothing for research at all. How does one respond to this dilemma?

First, one response to the dilemma is to realize that we are not dealing inherently with what is called a "zero sum" game. It is not true that money spent for research is subtracted from money that would otherwise go for services. In fact, most of the resources spent for research on family violence would probably not otherwise be spent for family violence at all. It would be spent on other kinds of research or on other problems entirely.

There is even another sense in which it is not a zero sum game. Even if research endeavors did subtract from service efforts in the short run, it is not true that they would in the long run. Research has, in the past, worked to give publicity and attention to problems that have in turn attracted new resources for services. But even more important, research has provided insights that have allowed a more efficient use of services, making it possible for money going into services to accomplish more. Nonetheless, the dilemma of research versus services, although perhaps not as simple as sometimes perceived, does have some reality. And it should be taken into account when making recommendations for research. One cannot, perhaps, be as frivolous in thinking about research in these fields as one can in others. Researchers need to keep the dilemma in mind. And one of the important criteria by which all research in this field should be judged is with this question: Are we confident that in the long run the results of this study will relieve or prevent as much suffering as an equivalent amount of money spent directly in services? We believe that for all the research proposed in this book, the answer to that question is yes.

Research on family violence poses other special ethical dilemmas, as well. The subjects of family violence research are not just ordinary people in everyday situations. They are people at special risk, in dangerous circumstances, who have suffered serious traumas and may well have psychological impairments. Any research done on family violence has a special responsibility to these individuals: a responsibility not to subject them to any additional trauma or contribute in any way to the perpetuation of their suffering. This places some limits on the types of research that can be done. As a result, we have included a special short review in this document of ethical issues of which all researchers, funding agencies, and policymakers must be aware. These concerns were very present in the consideration of each proposal. It is our belief that all the research proposed here can be done with the strictest protection of the rights and needs of victims of family violence.

What Is a Priority

Participating in this process has provided us much food for thought. Perhaps the most important question we have grappled with is what criteria one should apply in deciding whether a particular proposal is a priority. In answering that question, we have come to believe these factors should be taken into consideration.

(1) Scope of its impact. In comparing possible projects, some assessment needs to be made of which will have the greatest impact on the largest number of people. It is true that such a criteria does work to exclude projects related to small subpopulations. But a project the findings of which may benefit the situations of very large groups of people has an undeniable logic.

(2) Relevance of its findings. Studies are most relevant when they address issues of current public debate, and when they promise conclusions that will find application in the world of public policy. Sometimes priorities of this sort exclude speculative, theoretical, and basic kinds of research that can ultimately have even greater impact by challenging widely accepted assumptions and practices. But it is also true that research that has no audience and no constituency can easily be unnoticed and forgotten. In this field in which the policy needs are so great, research that directly addresses those burning policy issues must take some priority.

(3) Consensus among experts. In spite of the acrimonious debates that occur in this field, we were surprised at the number of proposals that were seen as priorities by practically everyone. A consensus on priorities, of course, can be misplaced. Sometimes it results from the disputes themselves rather than from a real policy need; everyone wants to see an issue tested because disagreements are so sharp. But that consensus also represents a great deal of collective thought and work and is thus worthy of some respect.

(4) Feasibility. This is a tricky criterion, and probably the least important of

the four. Many of the proposals given priority here have probably at one time or another been dismissed as unfeasible by a researcher or a funding agency. By feasibility, however, we do not primarily mean monetary feasibility. As we have indicated, there are other important constraints on family violence research, probably the most important being ethics. There have, unfortunately, been many ambitions projects in the field of family violence that simply never got off the ground because there was no ethical way to recruit subjects or no ethical way to test the intervention.

The priorities outlined in this document, we believe, are true to these criteria. They are feasible, relevant, seen as important by experts in the field, and capable of great impact on a large number of people.

2

A BRIEF HISTORY
OF FAMILY
VIOLENCE RESEARCH

Family violence research is an extremely young field. If one dates it back to the famous 1962 study by Henry Kempe and colleagues on the "Battered Child Syndrome," the field might be considered barely 25 years old. But even this exaggerates the field's maturity. In spite of the importance of the Kempe paper, it was still several years before it spawned additional study. A true "field" of research, consisting of more than some isolated reports, did not emerge until the early 1970s with publications like Gil's (1970) *Violence Against Children: Physical Abuse in the United States* and Steinmetz and Straus (1974) *Violence in the Family.*

It would be misleading to think, however, that the field of family violence research simply sprang from the new findings of social and medical scientists. Rather, the field grew up in conjunction with several historic social movements. In the 1960s, there began a large child welfare movement that championed the plight of abused and neglected children. In the 1970s, there was a powerful resurgence of the women's movement, which brought attention to the problem of battered wives. Both the women's movement and the child welfare movement were responsible for the sudden public spotlight on the problem of sexual abuse in the late 1970s. Although the social movements and the research findings nourished each other's growth, it would be most accurate to say that it was the social movements that posed the questions for which the researchers then went out and found the answers. Much less research would have been done, and much less attention paid to it, if there had not been expanding social movements concerning each of these problems.

In part because it was responding to these social forces, family violence research developed in discrete areas, in somewhat distinct eras. First came the research on physical child abuse in response to the child welfare concern of the late 1960s and early 1970s; then came the research on wife abuse, a reaction to the women's movement of the middle 1970s; this was followed by research on child sexual abuse in the late 1970s; and, finally, now in the mid-1980s, research on the family abuse of the elderly. However, within each topic area research progressed through some common patterns. Early attention to the problem would be focussed on primarily clinical case studies of the phenomenon. Kempe and Steele's early work (see Helfer & Kempe, 1974) on battered children received this attention, as did Martin's (1976) groundbreaking book on battered women, and also Burgess, Groth, Holmstrom, and Sgroi's (1978) work on the sexual abuse of children and adolescents. Meanwhile, other researchers were attempting to gather larger samples from agencies for the purposes of summarizing statistically the characteristics of the victims, offenders, and families. This would describe the early work of investigators such as Elmer (1967) on child abuse, Gelles (1974) on wife abuse, and Meiselman (1978) on sexual abuse.

As these fields developed, more sophisticated research strategies and designs quickly followed. A high priority was usually placed on developing some estimates of prevalence. These estimates were obtained from a variety of local and national surveys designed to identify cases that were not necessarily coming to public attention. Case comparison studies were also established, trying to differentiate families in which violence and abuse had occurred from others without such violence. And in some cases, longitudinal designs were applied, following either abusive or high-risk families for a time to test a variety of hypotheses.

The coalescence of a unified field called "family violence research" out of these disparate research endeavors has been slow and incomplete. It is a unity more emphasized by some researchers than others. However, a number of developments have helped bring the field together. The first national family violence research conference was held in 1981 at the University of New Hampshire, bringing together for the first time researchers concerned about child abuse, wife abuse, and sexual abuse. This conference was repeated in 1984 and in 1987. Another unifying force has been the publication of textbooks that considered the field as a whole. Steinmetz and Straus's *Violence in the Family* was such a landmark in early development and was the basis for many subsequent graduate and undergraduate courses on family violence. Pagelow's recent text, *Family Violence*, (1981) and Gelles and Pedrick Cornell, *Intimate Violence in Families* (1985), have carried on this tradition. Then, in 1985 and 1986, three new professional journals appeared that took as their focus family violence as a unity. These were the *Journal of Family Violence,* the *Journal of Interpersonal Violence,* and *Violence and Victims.* Finally, the federal government gave a boost to the unification of the field when the attorney general convened a task force on family violence, which published its recommendations in 1985, many of which called for additional research.

Of course, the emergence of an overarching field called "family violence research" has not changed the fact that within that field the level of development is quite uneven and fragmented. Child abuse research, which has the longest history, is perhaps the most advanced and sophisticated, and has the largest body of research findings, including a journal solely devoted to this subject (the *International Journal of Child Abuse and Neglect*). Work on child abuse is the central focus of a number of major research centers housed within major medical research facilities around the country, such as Children's Hospital in Boston and San Diego, and the University of Colorado Medical School. By contrast, elder abuse, the most recent entry into the field, is still in its infancy, with a few isolated investigators, mostly within social service agencies, studying this subject. As all the subfields mature, these differences become less conspicuous.

In the process of maturation, family violence research has drawn on the theories and methodologies of a number of other research traditions. Medicine, nursing, and public health, for example, have made major contributions, particularly to the child abuse field, with numerous studies from record reviews and studies utilizing prenatal and pediatric clinic populations. The field of family studies and family interaction has also made a contribution, providing instruments for observing and measuring parenting skills, and suggesting theories about why some families, like those with adolescent parents, may be more prone to violence. From another direction, developmental psychology has been an important resource, offering instruments for measuring the impact of abuse on children and designs for following up abused children over time. From still another tradition, criminology has greatly added to family violence research, suggesting techniques for gathering self-reports from abusers about their violent behavior. Finally, women's studies has played a crucial role, forwarding many theories about the nature and source of family violence.

The diversity of the traditions that have contributed to the field of family violence has been part of its strength. Each tradition has brought its own theories and methodologies, and through a process of "triangulation" a more complete picture of the phenomenon has emerged. But the diversity also poses special problems. Researchers from different traditions do not necessarily speak in the same research "language." They may not even have access to each other's work. Thus the diversity may have slowed and stymied the orderly and systematic accretion of knowledge in the field.

In spite of these obstacles, family violence has some impressive research accomplishments to boast for its short tenure. In three areas, quite a bit of research has been done: (1) A great deal is known about the prevalence of various types of family violence; (2) there is a fair bit of evidence about risk factors that are associated with family violence; and (3) a substantial body of knowledge exists concerning the effects of family violence on its victims. In the next section we will summarize briefly some of these findings.

THE PREVALENCE OF FAMILY VIOLENCE

Up until the last decade, family violence, to the extent that it was recognized, was generally considered an unusual problem that occurred mostly under extreme circumstances of family disorganization. One of the achievements of family violence research has been to demonstrate that family violence is quite widespread and occurs to some degree in almost all segments of society.

The task of measuring the prevalence of family violence has not been easy. For many years, policymakers and scientists were skeptical that good prevalence estimates were possible. Why would people truthfully reveal behaviors that were so embarrassing and shameful? Yet family violence researchers have combined sophisticated survey methodology with sensitive and careful interview techniques in such a way as to obtain the results many thought impossible.

The first prevalence estimates of child abuse were attempted in a national survey conducted by Gil (1970) in the late 1960s, in which a representative sample of Americans were asked about abusive incidents about which they may have known. However, it was not until 1975 that Straus, Gelles, and Steinmetz (1980) obtained estimates of child abuse and wife abuse based on a national survey in which family members were asked about their own experiences. In this study, 12% of the spouses said there had been an incident of violence between them in the previous year, while 28% said there had been a violent incident in the course of their marriage. Concerning abusive violence against children, 4% of the parents admitted to having used severe violence against their child in the previous year. These estimates led the researchers to extrapolate that there were close to two million abused wives and another two million abused children in the United States in 1975.

Prevalence studies of child sexual abuse have been somewhat slower to emerge. A landmark study in this area was one by Russell (1983), who questioned a representative sample of women in San Francisco. In this study, a remarkable 38% of the women recalled an incident of sexual abuse from their childhood; 18% reported such an incident at the hands of a family member. The first national study of sexual abuse was not conducted until 1985 by Lewis (Timnick, 1985), who found that 27% of the women and 15% of the men had been sexually abused as children. If rates like this were extrapolated to the current generation of children, it would imply about 700,000 new cases of sexual abuse every year.

Elder abuse, because of its short research history, has no national estimates yet. However, a recent study in the Boston metropolitan area by Pillemer and Finkelhor (1988) provided the first scientifically sound prevalence estimates for a locality. In this study, 3% of the elderly had suffered from one of three forms of abuse: physical violence, chronic verbal abuse, or neglect. If such a figure were to be found at a national level, it would extrapolate to close to a million abused elderly in the United States.

Researchers, in the course of some of these studies, uncovered previously hidden aspects of the family violence problem. For example, they demonstrated that in addition to being beaten, many wives were also sexually assaulted by husbands. Two community surveys suggested as many as 1 in 10 or 1 in 7 wives were raped or otherwise sexually abused by their partners (Finkelhor & Yllö, 1985; Russell, 1982). Researchers also suspected that the abusive behavior could be documented in the earliest stages of family formation, during the dating and courtship period. Following this lead, studies established that battering and sexual assault were as common in the courtship process as in later family life.

Besides demonstrating that a variety of different types of violence occurred in a large number of American families, these studies also clearly showed that no level of society is immune. In all the studies, for example, distressing rates of violence were found even in well-educated and affluent families, among the religious and nonreligious, and in both rural and urban areas. Child abuse and spouse abuse (but not sexual abuse) appear to be more common under conditions of economic stress, but they are by no means limited to these kinds of family situations. The picture of family violence as we know it today is a far cry from the picture we had even 15 years ago.

WHO IS AT RISK?

Family violence has been easier to count than to explain. It is clearly a problem with a diverse set of causes. Any comprehensive explanation will certainly require a consideration of specific family environments, child rearing practices, marital relationships, social attitudes, and social institutions, just to mention a few factors. Many ideas have been proposed, but family violence researchers are still far from agreement about how best to explain the different kinds of family violence. They have much greater consensus, however, about who is at risk. That is, they can state with some confidence types of individuals and families more likely to experience family violence. Although knowing who is at risk is not the same as knowing why they are at risk, it is useful. For example, it can form the basis for prevention programs aimed at reducing the amount of family violence by targeting certain vulnerable groups. If premature children are at higher risk, for example, as they may be, then this is a group that receives special attention.

Researchers have had the most experience and most success in identifying who is at risk for physical child abuse, in part because physically abusive families have been readily available to study from the caseloads of child protection agencies. Interestingly, the studies do not confirm the once-popular stereotype of child abusers as disturbed and malevolent individuals. Rather, they show abusers to be parents caught in highly stressful, unsupportive circumstances who have ineffective and unrealistic behaviors and attitudes surrounding child care.

The high-risk character of stressful environments has been well established. For example, low-income parents, teenage parents, parents without partners, and parents with unwanted children have all been demonstrated to have higher rates of abuse (Smith, 1984). Parents are also more likely to abuse when caring for a child who has special needs because of illness, congenital defect, or temperament. Social isolation—being cut off from family, neighborhood, or institutional supports—is another important stress-related risk factor (Garbarino, 1976).

Physical child abusers have also been demonstrated to have ineffective and conflict-prone styles of parenting. They have inappropriate expectations of children, they are overly reactive in their dealings with children, and they have difficulty rewarding children for good behavior (Wolfe, 1985). The fact that they are more likely to have themselves been subject to harsh and abusive treatment as children (Straus et al., 1980) suggests from where their own patterns have come.

The risk factors for physical child abuse are sufficiently well understood now that several researchers have been able to create tests to identify potential child abusers (Bavolek, 1984; Milner & Wimberly, 1980). These tests have proven to be very useful in research and prevention (for example, they are used in high school programs to teach parenting skills to teenagers), and they demonstrate some of the payoffs of research that tries to identify risk factors.

By comparison, much less is known about the risk factors behind child sexual abuse, but they are clearly not the same as those for physical abuse. For example, poverty and economic stress have not been shown to increase the risk for sexual abuse as they do for physical abuse (Finkelhor & Baron, 1986). Unfortunately, many other possible factors that may increase risk have simply not been tested, in part because sexual abusers have been generally less available and cooperative with research efforts. But retrospective studies from grown-up victims looking back at their childhood have revealed the importance of several family conditions.

Children appear to be at greater risk to sexual abuse, for example, when their natural father is gone from their home and especially when they are living with a stepfather. They are also at higher risk when they have a difficult relationship with their mother because mother is either sick, incapacitated, or emotionally unavailable. If the parents' marriage is full of conflict, this also seems to put children at risk (Finkelhor & Baron, 1986). Why these are risk factors is not entirely clear. These seem to be factors that lead to emotional deprivation and poor supervision and this seems how they are connected to higher vulnerability.

In regard to wife abuse, the rapid accumulation of new studies in the early 1980s now seems to be paying off for researchers in the form of some firm conclusions. After some years of controversy, they are finally being able to spotlight certain risk factors as key while dismissing others as irrelevant (Hotaling & Sugarman, 1986). An important conclusion seems to be that there is little that distinguishes the battered wife from other women. Ideas, once popular, that such women had low self-esteem, or traditional notions regarding sex roles or other personality characteristics, have not been substantiated. Instead, all indicators point to characteristics of the husband as being the best predictors.

The picture of battering men now put together by numerous research studies is of individuals with extensive patterns of maladjustment and antisocial behavior (Hotaling & Sugarman, 1986). Batterers are more likely to be of low educational attainment, low income and low occupational status. They are more likely to have low self-esteem, low levels of assertiveness, and little sense of personal efficacy. And they are substantially more likely to have a history of sexual aggressiveness, violence toward others (including their children), and, in some studies, police records. One of the most consistently replicated findings is that batterers, as children and adolescents, were the witnesses to violence and abuse in their families of origin.

Interestingly, some other presumptions about batterers have not been consistently confirmed (Hotaling & Sugarman, 1986). Studies have not found batterers to necessarily have traditional sex-role expectations, or unusual needs for power and dominance. It almost goes without saying, however, that their marriages are high in conflict and argument and low in marital satisfaction.

EFFECTS OF FAMILY VIOLENCE

In addition to risk factors, researchers have in recent years been increasingly able to document the extensive consequences of family violence. The portrait is of a problem the effects of which radiate in many directions for an extended period of time and touch the lives of many others besides the perpetrator and the immediate victim.

The physical consequences of family violence, being the most obvious and immediate, have been among those most easy to document. Death, the most serious of these, is more common than many people recognize. According to FBI statistics for 1984, for example, 24% of all homicides were committed against family members. A total of 730 children were killed by parents, 504 parents by children, 403 siblings by siblings, and 2,116 spouses by spouses (Straus, 1986). Moreover, it is generally recognized that a certain proportion of family homicides (especially of very young children killed by parents) escape detection and are classified as accidental deaths.

The toll of nonfatal physical injury is also great. For example, among battered women who seek help from shelters, 80% to 90% have been injured, and among those who call the police this is true for 23% to 66% (Bowen, Straus, Sedlak, Hotaling, & Sugarman, 1984). In surveys of the general population, an estimated 9% to 12% of the women who report a violent incident with a spouse in the previous year say they had to seek medical attention. Children, because they are small, are particularly vulnerable to physical effects from abuse. Major injuries (brain damage, skull fracture, subdural hematoma, bone fracture, dislocation, internal injury, burn) are reported by about 13% of all physically abused children, and minor injuries (cuts, bruises) by another 72% (AAPC, 1986). Studies indicate that children who have been abused are at increased risk for neurological impairment, developmental deficits, and generally poorer physical health (Elmer & Gregg, 1967; Lynch & Roberts, 1982; Martin, Beezley, Conway, & Kempe, 1974).

The evidence has also been accumulating about the long-term mental health impact of family violence. The conclusion is now inescapable that histories of family violence occur in disproportionate amounts among those who are suffering from a large variety of mental health problems. A recent study of hospitalized psychiatric patients, for example, found that 39% reported a history of family violence (Carmen, Rieker, & Mills, 1984). Two recent surveys of mental health status in the general population (one in Los Angeles and one in Calgary) showed that those who had a history of child sexual abuse were over twice as likely to have a range of psychiatric disturbances, from depression and anxiety to drug abuse, and were also twice as likely as others to have sought mental health treatment (Bagley & Ramsay, 1986; Siegel, Burnam, Stein, Goldberg, & Sorenson, 1986).

Research on wife abuse and physical and sexual child abuse show all leading to some common patterns of mental health impairment. The victims suffering from the long-term effects of abuse are characterized by low self-esteem, instability in their intimate relationships, anxiety, depression, suicide attempts, substance abuse, psychosomatic complaints, and poor functioning in school and work situations (Bowen et al., 1984; Browne & Finkelhor, 1986; Martin et al., 1974). These common symptom patterns seem related to common elements in the abusive situation: betrayal and continual denigration by trusted figures, a sense of powerlessness to stop the abuse, and the experience of isolation and social stigma. Many victims of family violence, especially in its more severe forms, show symptoms characteristic of post-traumatic stress disorder (PTSD)—including diffuse anxiety, intrusive recollections of traumatic events, and deadening of affective response (Eth & Pynoos, 1985; Figley, 1985).

In addition to some of these common symptoms, there are also certain symptoms that seem to be specific to particular types of family violence. For example, victims of sexual abuse appear to suffer, not surprisingly, from long-term problems in the area of sexual functioning. They are more likely than nonvictims to report aversion to sex or promiscuous sexual behavior, and they are also at high risk to be sexually victimized in some other way at a later time. Victims of physical child abuse, for their part, seem to be at particularly high risk to suffer intellectual impairment, especially difficulties in the development of language skills (Lynch & Roberts, 1982). The school difficulties of physically abused children are particularly prominent, including the high risk of becoming a behavior problem in school.

Perhaps the most sinister aspect of family violence, however, is its self-perpetuating character. Victims of family violence seem to be at higher risk to become both future victims and future perpetrators. The inevitability of this connection is sometimes exaggerated in popular discussion. Abused children are by no means *destined* to grow up to become abusive parents. In fact, to many people's surprise, most do not (Herrenkohl, Herrenkohl, & Toedter, 1983). However, the risk of becoming an abusive parent is substantially higher for an abused child than it is for some other child. And this is the fact behind the notion of a cycle of abuse.

Researchers have found support for a cycle of abuse on a number of fronts. Parents who were themselves subject to severe physical punishment are more than twice as likely to subject their own children to such treatment (Straus et al., 1980). Husbands who witnessed their fathers beat their mothers are more than twice as likely to beat their wives (Hotaling & Sugarman, 1986). In fact, witnessing violence in one's family of origin is the most consistently demonstrated background factor among wife abusers, more common than being a victim of child abuse, another factor that has been confirmed in a number of studies.

The cycle also seems to operate such that victimization can lead to further victimization. For example, girls who were sexually abused as children are more likely to grow up to be battered wives (Russell, 1986). Women who were sexually abused as children may also be more likely to have daughters who are abused (Goodwin, McCarthy, & DiVasto, 1981).

Moreover, the transmission of violence is not confined within the family. There is research evidence that family violence can lead to violence in other settings as well. For example, delinquents and violent criminals have been shown in numerous studies to have had more child abuse in their backgrounds (McCord, 1983; Hunner & Walker, 1981).

The cycle of violence makes intuitive sense, perhaps the reason it is sometimes used to explain more about family violence than it really does. People learn how to conduct intimate relationships through the models they have. Certainly if you have seen others use violence to handle conflict and frustration, it will seem a more plausible and legitimate answer when you too encounter difficulties. If you have suffered family violence, you may also be more tolerant of its use by others, against both yourself and your children. However, the cycle is certainly more complex than this. To the extent that those who are abused suffer from a sense of powerlessness, stigma, and a difficulty in trusting others, their healthy coping resources are impaired. Violence is an ultimate resource, a tactic of powerlessness and desperation.

But the cycle is even more complex in that many people escape it. The less publicized finding of research is that most victims of family violence do not grow up to be perpetrators or victims. Many take from their experiences a strong commitment never to inflict such anguish on others. How people recover from the trauma of abuse is not well understood. It is one of the major tasks of future research.

RESEARCH ON POLICIES
TO DEAL WITH FAMILY VIOLENCE

Some of the most pressing questions concern how to respond to family violence, yet it is in this area that research has been most conspicuously lacking. For the most part, the need to react quickly to the crisis of family violence has created conditions not well suited to the carrying out of careful evaluation research.

Nonetheless, there have been some important efforts to study the different kinds of intervention strategies used in dealing with family violence. Although the findings of these studies have not always received the attention they deserved, they have provided interesting conclusions. And they have served as models for kinds of efforts that might be made in the future.

For example, the federal government on several occasions has funded researchers to do comparative evaluations of child abuse treatment programs that are using a variety of approaches in a variety of locales around the country. Although the findings of these efforts have been subject to many criticisms, there were a few conclusions on which they appeared to agree (Daro & Cohn, 1984). For example, certain services provided to abusive parents, particularly the nonprofessional ones like Parents Anonymous, appeared particularly effective. Also group services, like group therapy and parent education classes, proved especially promising.

A study that had particularly important policy implications for the field of wife abuse was the Minneapolis police experiment (Sherman & Berk, 1984). This study compared the effectiveness of three different methods for handling domestic disturbance calls: (1) arresting the abuser, (2) providing arbitration for the couple, (3) simply separating the couple. The study found that arresting the abuser resulted in a significant reduction in the amount of further abuse that was reported. Police departments around the country, citing these findings, have begun to adopt mandatory arrest policies in cases of wife abuse.

General Problems of Family Violence Research

In spite of the foregoing accomplishments, there are still many intrinsic problems in the field of family violence research. These problems—concerning definitions, methodology, and ethical concerns—continue to plague the field and have rarely been addressed directly. Rather researchers have come to accept them and carry on their work in spite of them.

Problems with Definitions

There are profound disagreements and uncertainties concerning how to delimit the key objects of study in this field. A prime example is spanking. Spanking is an extremely widespread practice in American society, utilized by over 90% of all parents, and regarded as normative—and, in fact, positive—by most lay people. Almost no professional would label moderate spanking as child abuse. Yet spanking is certainly a form of "family violence." Violence is usually defined as the use of force to intentionally inflict pain. The infliction of pain is certainly the intention of spanking. True, it is usually pain administered for what is seen as a "good reason," but so are warfare and police actions, which are clearly violent.

So there has been question about whether spanking should really be counted and studied as a form of family violence. For the most part, family violence researchers have chosen to study it, but as a special case. They have treated it as a phenomenon in and of itself and have not lumped it together with more serious kinds of violence against children. When tallying up the "problem" of family violence they do not include it in the "body count." But this is not completely satisfactory either. Researchers and professionals know that some forms of spanking are abusive, and they know that many forms of child abuse occur in the context of what the abusers believe to be simple physical punishment. Many researchers are also personally opposed to physical punishment and agree with the Swedish government, which has decided that it is an unhealthy practice that encourages abuses and declared it illegal. So spanking and physical punishment are controversial subjects in which scientists, policymakers, and lay people are still doing battle and trying to sort out the evidence. As a result, its status has not clearly been delineated in the field of family violence.

There are other such classification problems, especially with regard to what are seen as less serious types of family violence—for example, fights between siblings, or occasional pushes, slaps, and shoves in marital relationships. Then there are also issues about what a family is; does it include "paramours," such as in the case of the mother's boyfriend who molests her children. There is also the question of whether nonviolent forms of maltreatment—emotional abuse, physical neglect—should be included in the field. All these are examples of unresolved definitional problems in the field of family violence.

Problems in Gathering Data

For a field of study to exist and grow, researchers must have the tools to be able to identify and have access to their main object of study. An astronomer living underground who receives pictures from above in which he cannot distinguish between the stars and the streetlamps is in a sad state indeed. However, family violence researchers are in just such a state. Unfortunately, most family violence occurs in private. Very little of it is witnessed by other than the participants, and almost never by researchers. Researchers must rely on accounts given by participants, and unfortunately the validity of these accounts are difficult to ascertain. Family violence is stigmatizing and shameful. It occurs under circumstances of heated emotions and in relationships characterized by conflict, frustration, and bitterness. So it is likely that many people who experience family violence will not admit to it. It is also likely that those who do admit to it will give accounts that are affected and perhaps distorted by their own powerful emotional needs.

The questions this raises are very troubling. Almost all cases of family violence are identified in two ways, neither of them very satisfying. On the one hand, social agencies identify individuals who have been involved in family violence. The process by which social agencies make this identification is very fallible. Most of the individuals labeled resist the labelling. It is widely agreed that reported cases of family violence are but a small portion of actually occurring cases and are biased in ways that have to do with prejudices and processes of the agencies involved. On the other hand, family violence is identified outside of agencies by independent researchers who recruit self-identified victims and perpetrators. It is believed that here too much family violence is missed, and it is virtually impossible to determine how much, since the only way to validate questionable self-reports is with other questionable self-reports.

It is true that family violence researchers have made some progress on these issues. In the beginning, social scientists doubted that one could gather self-report data on family violence at all. But techniques have developed that have been more successful in gaining admissions than even the developers imagined. However, little further research has been conducted on the validity of these self-reports. It raises the possibility that much of what we have learned about family violence is based on distortions.

Absence of Institutionalized Data Collection

Social phenomena can be divided into those that are subject to *systematic* and those that are subject to *unsystematic* data collection. Systematic data collection is provided for such things as automobile accidents, communicable diseases, unemployed persons, rapes reported to the police, annual income, and so forth. In these cases, large-scale organized systems have been established to collect uniform information on a regular basis on these phenomena. The collection systems are called such things as the Census, the Uniform Crime Report, the Survey of Business Statistics, and so forth.

Family violence, for the most part, is subject to no such systematic data collection. There are two exceptions. Child abuse statistics are collected annually by individual states. Some effort has been made by the American Humane Association to systematize these reports and turn them into national statistics, but this effort has been unsuccessful in gaining the participation of all states, and is not assured of continued existence. In one other exception, some family violence data is gathered by the criminal justice system, since crimes of family violence are included in the crimes covered by the Uniform Crime Reports and the National Crime Survey. However, both these surveys have been criticized for excluding large amounts of family violence, and neither reports statistics in ways that allow easily for the analysis of family violence as a discrete phenomenon.

The absence of systematically collected data on family violence is a serious obstacle for the field. When data on a subject are systematically collected, researchers can monitor historical changes; they can correlate rates of the phenomenon with those of other related phenomena; they can look for regional, demographic, and social class relationships. At the current moment, such analyses in the field of family violence are possible only at infrequent intervals. The Center for Disease Control has explored the possibility of trying to establish a systematic data collection system for domestic violence. However, no immediate plans are in the works for the implementation of such a system. The National Crime Survey has also discussed the possibility of gathering more systematic family violence data. The outcome of these discussions is currently unknown.

CONCLUSION

In spite of these challenges, family violence research has recorded some important achievements in its short history. It has greatly contributed to awareness about the problem by documenting its scope and its impact. It has sensitized professionals and the public to aspects of the problem—like marital rape, adolescent sexual abusers—that were poorly recognized and not well understood. It has identified certain risk factors that can be utilized in identifying those at greatest likelihood to become victims and perpetrators.

These are not "discoveries" that add up to a "cure." But they are achievements that show promise. As the field gains momentum, adds investigators, and conquers some problems of methodology, the possibility is great that further research will contribute measurably to the reduction in the toll of family violence.

PREFACE TO THE PROPOSALS

It is very unusual in the professional or scientific literature to see a lengthy inventory of research projects such as this. So a brief introduction is warranted to explain the format and prepare the reader for what is to come.

The three chapters to follow contain agendas of 11 to 14 proposals, each described in a page or two. These proposals were the end product of the process described in the introduction—a selection and melding of several dozen ideas from several dozen researchers. They are listed in rough order of priority, based on the scoring of these same consultants. However, differences in scores between adjacent proposals was sometimes small, and no great significance should be given to the exact ordering. Moreover, there were many excellent suggestions for projects that did not make this list. The absence of a subject from the agenda does not by any means imply that it was considered unimportant.

The descriptions of each project were designed with several considerations in mind. We wished them to be detailed enough to give researchers a clear idea of the kinds of methodologies that were being proposed, without at the same time getting bogged down in technical issues that might be too detailed for those with a general policy interest and too distracting for researchers because they would provoke unnecessary argument. We wanted the description to make a strong case about why such a project was important and give researchers, funders, and policymakers a sense of the contribution such a project would make.

The exact details of each project, however, are in no ways sacrosanct. For example, other researchers might develop equally valid ways of drawing samples. Follow-up periods could generally be adjusted to be shorter or longer, depending on funding that is available. Moreover, many of these studies could easily be broken up into small substudies. Some of the proposals presented here really are conglomerations of two or three separate suggestions, put together so as to be able to include all of them. With a smaller amount of money or a shorter time period, it would be easy enough to do only a part of one of the suggested studies.

Finally, a word needs to be said about the cost estimates; they are very gross and rough approximations, meant simply to convey an order of magnitude. Depending on specifics many of these studies could be done for anywhere from half to twice the estimate given here.

3

HIGH PRIORITY RESEARCH ON PHYSICAL CHILD ABUSE

1. Evaluating Physical Abuse Prevention Strategies
2. The Long Term Effects of Child Abuse
3. Evaluating Alternatives in Child Protection
4. Physically Abusive Fathers
5. The Dynamics of Anger Arousal in Families
6. Child Abuse Mistaken for Accidental Deaths
7. Public Attitudes Toward Corporal Punishment
8. Improving the Child Abuse Substantiation Process
9. Improving Methodologies to Detect Child Abuse
10. The Economic Costs of Child Abuse
11. State Data for Evaluating the Effectiveness of Child Welfare Policies

Of the three forms of family violence under consideration in this report, physical child abuse was the first to be publicly and professionally recognized. Thus the research tradition in this field extends back further than any of the others, covering a period of nearly 25 years. In spite of this lengthy heritage, the research record is spotty. On some matters, such as identifying parents at risk to abuse, a great deal of work has been done. On other matters, such as the economic cost of child abuse, little or nothing exists. Thus the priorities proposed here reflect a mixture of the advanced and the exploratory. Some seek to test proposals that have been the product of prior research and development. Some rest on substantial prior practical and theoretical achievement. Others push back the frontiers on matters about which little is still known.

1. EVALUATING PHYSICAL ABUSE PREVENTION STRATEGIES

This priority consists of several studies that would evaluate the effectiveness of such programs as parent education, home visiting, emergency day care, and child allowances to see how well they reduce the likelihood that high-risk families will abuse their young children.

Need and Rationale

There is broad agreement among experts in the field that the top priority should be given to evaluating programs—like parent home visitation programs—that are designed to prevent parents from physically abusing their young (ages 0 to 3) children. The consensus behind this priority stems from several factors. First, the abuse of young children is an extremely serious type of child abuse the consequences of which not infrequently include either death or lifelong physical and psychological impairment.

Second, as a result of much prior research in this area, the causes of this kind of abuse are fairly well understood and include the social and physical isolation of parents, poverty, social stress, single-parenthood, unrealistic expectations of the child, emotional immaturity, and inadequate knowledge about parenting (Starr, 1982). Since so much is understood, the potential for effective impact is great.

Third, a number of demonstration projects, working with groups of high-risk parents, have appeared successful (both in the opinion of their directors and in small-scale evaluations). It is timely at the moment to build on these successes by confirming and elaborating their results.

For these and other reasons, many experts are optimistic that a major research initiative could unambiguously and comprehensively demonstrate the effectiveness of prevention, and thus become the starting place for a broad new social policy that would curtail one of the most serious forms of child abuse.

Unfortunately, although agreed about the importance of evaluating prevention programs, experts are divided about just exactly what to evaluate. There appear to be roughly two schools of thought. The first urges a study of the one approach that has the greatest likelihood of success in order to clearly establish that prevention is feasible and worthy of further implementation and study. In this case, the most promising program is generally seen as the professional home visitor program, in which high-risk, disadvantaged mothers are regularly visited by a professional who gives them social and community support and teaches them child care skills. At least two studies have suggested some success for this kind of approach (Olds et al., 1986; Gray et al., 1977).

However, another school of thought urges a much more comprehensive type of prevention research. Proponents of this school believe there are many promising approaches to prevention that may be as or more effective than home visitation but simply have not been evaluated as extensively. They would like studies to evaluate a variety of different prevention programs including:

— home visiting conducted not just by professionals but also by nonprofessionals, such as neighborhood volunteers or the elderly
— parent education classes during prenatal and postnatal periods that help impart to parents better parenting skills, including better nurturing and support skills for fathers
— parent support groups in which parents learn skills and share problems with other parents
— the provision of free, high-quality day care, for both regular and emergency situations, so that any parent under stress can get relief from child care burdens without prior notice
— increased financial support for new parents, which might take the form of a governmental "child allowance"

Unless such a variety of programs is evaluated, this school believes there may be a premature selection of only one approach, when others are actually more efficient and effective.

The differences between the two schools of thought concerning how prevention studies should be done are not really fundamental. They are based more on political and economic considerations and on the presumption that only one major prevention evaluation study, if any, is going to be undertaken in the immediate future. The disagreement would evaporate if many studies were planned. The solution then is to undertake at least two and perhaps several prevention evaluation studies, one evaluating the home visitor program and one or several evaluating and comparing other programs.

Goals

All of these studies should have similar goals and similar formats. The goals should be: first, to demonstrate that prevention programs do work to reduce child abuse; second, to provide some assessment of the relative costs and benefits of the programs; third, to specify the types of approaches that are the most effective and efficient; and finally, to specify for whom and under what conditions these programs work the best.

Design Considerations

To best implement these goals, these evaluation studies should try to incorporate some of these features:

(1) The studies should assign families to the various alternative prevention programs in such a way as to create equivalent test groups. They must guard against the possibility that more motivated or healthier families get chosen for one particular program.

(2) The studies should be carried out on diverse populations of vulnerable families—including rural and urban families; black, white, and Hispanic families; single-parent and two-parent families—in order to match programs with the populations for which they may be the most effective.

(3) In addition to reporting on short-term (1- to 2-year) effectiveness, the studies need to follow up the families for a substantial period, at least 5 and possibly as many as 10 years. Interim findings will be useful for policymakers. But only through a long follow-up can the full impact of prevention be seen, something particularly important in terms of calculating the costs and benefits.

Conclusion

These are ambitious undertakings. But experts are convinced that we are close to demonstrating real results in efforts to prevent child abuse. This warrants substantial commitment to this project.

Summary

Time Needed: 3 to 10 years
Cost: $1.5 to $2.0 million

2. THE LONG-TERM EFFECTS
OF CHILD ABUSE

This study is a longitudinal study of abused children until they reach adulthood to examine the effects of abuse on mental health, delinquency, and school performance, and to understand the factors associated with recovery from the trauma of abuse.

Need and Rationale

Child abuse appears to lead to a variety of other very serious social problems: delinquency, crime, mental illness, mental retardation, and teenage pregnancy. If these connections are strong, it might be argued, as some indeed have, that *child abuse prevention is the most important way to prevent many other social problems.* A study confirming these connections in a way convincing to the public and policymakers could have an enormous impact on the field. It could greatly broaden the public, professional, and political support for action on child abuse.

The belief that child abuse leads to other social problems already does have some solid research support. That research includes studies showing high rates of abuse in the backgrounds of various troubled populations, such as juvenile delinquents (Hunner & Walker, 1981), criminals (McCord, 1983), and psychiatric patients (Carmen, Rieker, & Mills, 1984). But these studies do not prove that child abuse is responsible for later problems, nor do they answer many of the serious questions about the long-term impact of child abuse.

Goals

These are some of the outstanding issues that should be looked at:

(1) Can we document not only that abused children have a significantly greater risk of delinquency, criminal careers, and other antisocial behavior, but also that it is the abuse, rather than some other background factor—such as poverty, or parental criminality, or the neighborhood subculture—that is responsible for this outcome? Many professionals in the child abuse field have contended that child abuse treatment was one of the most effective approaches to crime prevention. Because the public is so preoccupied with crime, strong scientific support for this contention could greatly bolster public support for all types of child abuse prevention and treatment activities.

(2) What types of maltreatment are associated with what types of long-term effects? For example, is abuse by fathers connected more to criminality and abuse by mothers to mental illness? This question is important for a better understanding of how the trauma of child abuse operates. The answer will help practitioners to anticipate some of the consequences of different types of abuse and fashion their interventions in a way that will be maximally therapeutic.

A specific form of this question concerns the relationship between physical and psychological abuse. Some researchers have raised the possibility that the traumatic effects of child abuse are not due to the physical violence so much as the psychological abuse—the denigration, threats, emotional manipulation, hostility—that accompany it. Although these two types of abusiveness are frequently so interconnected that it is difficult to disentangle them, it can be done, particularly by looking at groups of children who suffered the psychological abuse without the violence. The findings would have important implications for treatment.

(3) How does the impact of abuse differ on different groups of children? For example, boys and girls have different long-term reactions to abuse. Is it true in the long-term that girls are more likely to suffer depression, suicide, and running away? It is also important to understand the different effects of being abused and being a witness to siblings who are abused.

(4) Why do many abused children appear to recover from their childhood traumas? We know from personal histories that there are many adults who become well-functioning and successful in spite of having grown up with abuse. Not much is known, except in a very general way, about what works to promote such recovery from the trauma. For example, when children take active roles in the reporting of their abuse and in the interventions that occur, do they have more positive outcomes? When children are able to develop close relationships with other adults as substitute role models for abusing parents, does this contribute to recovery? If the recovery processes could be documented in a very specific way, among people who never received any formal intervention as well as those who did, it would be of enormous value in designing treatment programs for abused children. Programs could be devised to try to replicate the process of recovery identified in the well-functioning victims.

Design Considerations

To answer these kinds of questions, what is needed is a large-scale longitudinal study of abused children (and some siblings), following them from when they were first identified until maturity, paying close attention to both healthy and pathological outcomes. A definitive study should contain some of the following components:

(1) A large sample and diverse variety of abused children. For example, the study might look for 1,000 children from a variety of jurisdictions. The children should include those from middle-class as well as lower-class environments, different racial and ethnic backgrounds, and those who suffered very serious as well as less serious forms of abuse.

(2) Follow-up should be planned for at least 15 years to allow most of the abused children to grow into late adolescence or early adulthood. However, children could be evaluated as often as every 3 years. This would allow the study to collect interim data on life events that may contribute to recovery (or deterioration). It would also provide inter-mediate outcome reports from which to draw tentative conclusions.

(3) The study should take care to get very complete information on children's interim functioning. This should include assessment of the children's intellectual, cognitive, academic, and social performance. Parents and teachers should be interviewed and a review made of juvenile court and police records for evidence of delinquent or criminal behavior on the part of the children.

Conclusion

A large-scale and ambitious study of this sort would provide a major impetus for a wider public policy recognition of the serious consequences of child abuse and the possibility of short-circuiting some of the most severe detrimental outcomes.

Summary

Time needed:	5 to 15 years
Cost:	$800,000
Special problems:	keeping track of children and following them up after many years

3. EVALUATING ALTERNATIVES IN CHILD PROTECTION

This is a study of the relative impact on children of five different options for dealing with children who need protection from abusive parents.

Need and Rationale

Child protection work entails difficult choices, made without sufficient information. Among the most difficult, for example, is whether to remove children from parental custody in situations where there is no adult capable of providing protection. Separated from the abusers, many argue, children are much more securely protected from the possibility of reabuse. But others worry that in this condition children are also separated from their familiar surroundings, from the people they know and love. There is a heated debate about whether the concern about maintaining the family unit is a rationale social policy or an nostalgic commitment to obsolete traditional values.

Unfortunately, the assumptions that underlie this policy dilemma have been subjected only infrequently to scientific study. How much harm does separation from family cause the child? Do children left in families in which they are moderately abused fare better in the long run than equivalent children who were removed? How serious does the risk for reabuse need to be before it justifies removing the child? Are there some combinations of family intervention that can be safely substituted for a decision to remove the child in many circumstances? All these are questions that can be approached scientifically. Their answers could have a dramatic impact on the practice of hundreds of child protective agencies and the fate of thousands of children.

Goals

What is needed is a systematic follow-up and evaluation of abused children who are subject to various types of intervention by child protective agencies. At least four different intervention patterns should be contrasted to each other: (1) removal of the child from home in a manner typical of many child welfare agencies; (2) removal of the child from the home in conjunction with an unusual, intensive intervention to minimize the trauma of removal; (3) allowing the child to remain in the family along with a typical pattern of child protection intervention (casework, family services, etc.); (4) allowing the child to remain in the family along with an unusual, intensive program of assistance to family. With these four conditions we would be able to contrast the effect of removing or leaving the child in the home, but also be able to see the effect of providing an intensive intervention in either case. Thus it might turn out that removing the child was preferable to leaving the child under conditions typical of most child protective intervention, but not preferable to leaving the child with intensive intervention. This would tell child welfare policymakers that if they wished to avoid removing children while still protecting them to the maximum degree, the alternative would be to provide a more intensive package of services.

Design Considerations

Although the theory behind this type of study has a great deal of appeal, its implementation poses some very difficult problems. Rarely is it possible to derive any conclusions by comparing children left in abusive families with those removed, because the removed children are almost always a much more seriously abused and disturbed group; this is why they are removed. Under ideal scientific conditions, children would be randomly assigned to each intervention, creating four initially equal groups. But no real world researcher could ethically perform such an experiment.

Two strategies are possible, however, that could overcome the problem of nonequivalent groups subjected to each intervention. The first would use some systematic assignment, the second compare different jurisdictions. Under most circumstances, assignment of abused children is unethical because of clear indications that some children need to be removed, and in other cases because of clear indications that removal would be unnecessarily drastic. But these clearcut cases are not the ones that most need study. It is the ambiguous ones in which policymakers need help. Child welfare authorities could certainly identify a fairly large group of cases in which everyone was in agreement that there was truly a dilemma about which course to take. The study could be limited to this "dilemma group" and essentially allow some portion of them to be assigned to interventions on a systematic basis that would create equivalent groups in each condition.

Another possibility for design of such a study is to take advantage of the fact that child welfare practice differs a great deal across the country. Some jurisdictions remove children from abusers at much higher rates than others. Using fairly detailed criteria concerning the child, the family, and the type of abuse, cases could be identified in each jurisdiction that are very similar in form but very different in disposition. Psychological evaluations of the child prior to disposition could be used to further ensure that the children are equivalent. A follow-up and comparison of these children would allow researchers to contrast the relative merits of removing children versus leaving them with abusive parents.

Conclusion

This is a potentially very important study. It holds the possibility of relieving some of the intense uneasiness and riskiness to the practice of child protection by putting its principles on a more scientific foundation.

Summary

Time needed:	5 to 10 years
Cost:	$800,000
Special problems:	finding a system that would implement the study

4. PHYSICALLY ABUSIVE FATHERS

This priority is a proposal for data from both old and new studies on fathers who commit child abuse.

Need and Rationale

About half of all physical abuse is committed by fathers. But most studies of child abusers have focused on women. Judith Martin (1983), reviewing 76 studies in 1980, found that only 2 had focused exclusively on men, compared to 31 focused on women. Those studying both men and women rarely made distinctions based on gender, although this may be crucial. The reasons why fathers abuse may be very different from the reasons why mothers do. Having a history of violent behavior may be a more important factor with fathers. Job loss and job dissatisfaction may be another important ingredient. Attitudes of entitlement and belief in absolute patriarchal authority may be still another. More study is needed of the specific elements related to abuse by fathers.

Goals

Some of these questions need answers:

(1) How are the dynamics of abuse by fathers different from those of abuse by mothers? For example, it has been found that men are more likely to abuse teenagers and less likely than women to abuse infants (Garbarino et al., 1986; Straus et al., 1980). Are there also differences in the degree of injuries inflicted? In the likelihood of recidivism?

(2) How do abusive fathers differ from abusive mothers in terms of backgrounds, attitudes, and motivations for abusing? Are abusive fathers more likely to have had a history of previous violent behavior? Are abusive fathers more likely to believe in strict discipline and absolute parental authority? Are abusive fathers more likely to abuse in a deliberate, nonangry way?

(3) Men in general have less experience in nurturing and acquire fewer parenting skills before becoming a parent. Is there a close relationship between having such experiences and skills and their likelihood to abuse?

(4) Fathers are particularly likely to abuse their teenage and pre-teenage daughters. How much of the physical abuse by men is connected to sexual abuse or to their attempting to cope with sexual feelings toward their daughters?

(5) When men abuse children they also often abuse their spouses. Why would some men be violent toward spouses and not children, and vice

versa? What does this tell us about the inhibition of violence in family relationships among otherwise violence-prone men?

Design Considerations

To answer some of these questions, two studies are needed. A first step is to go back to the dozens of studies that have been done with physical child abusers of both sexes and to reanalyze that data with particular attention to the fathers and their differences from the mothers. A great deal of information is already available but simply has not been gleaned because investigators were not interested specifically in abusive fathers. The second step is to undertake new studies of abusive men.

Conclusion

These studies will help to solve the other, missing half of the child abuse puzzle, and thus help us to design programs that can work in preventing abuse by men as well as women.

Summary

Time needed:	3 years
Cost:	$300,000
Special problems:	obtaining representative samples of abusive fathers since they are less likely to be involved in treatment programs

5. THE DYNAMICS OF
ANGER AROUSAL IN FAMILIES

This priority proposes studies in laboratory and real family situations of how family members become angry at one another and how these situations resolve themselves, in order to understand how to inhibit anger and its subsequent turning into violence and abuse.

Need and Rationale

Most researchers in the field of physical child abuse recognize a connection between abuse and anger: In most cases anger precedes the abuse. But the details of the connection are not clear. Why doesn't anger always lead to violence? Is anger reduction a good approach to violence reduction? Anger and aggression have been extensively studied in laboratory conditions. Much less is known about anger in child-rearing situations, and this is where we need to generalize our knowledge.

Goals

The study should answer these kinds of questions: What behavior in children is most likely to prompt parental anger? What factors act to inhibit that anger—for example, the presence of other adults, the responses of the child, beliefs about the inappropriateness of anger? What factors act to exacerbate the anger—fatigue, stress, the persistence of the child's noxious behavior? Under what conditions does an angry parent become a violent parent? How do a person's beliefs about what is appropriate and what is expected affect their likelihood of becoming angry and of allowing that anger to become violent? How are these dynamics different in fathers and mothers, in parents of different social classes, or in parents with different attitudes toward physical punishment? The study needs to consider both the instigating factors to anger and violence as well as all the inhibiting factors.

Design Considerations

Two types of studies need to be conducted: one in the laboratory and one in actual families. There is an extensive body of research on family interaction performed in laboratory settings, but little of it on anger (Gottman, 1979). There is also an extensive body of research on anger, but little on it with families. Detailed studies of the interactions patterns in abusive families can be done, as illustrated by the work of Burgess and Conger (1978), Patterson (1982), and Reid (1986). Some of the studies from the social psychological literature on anger arousal need to be redone in the laboratory with parents and children to see how the dynamics differ. However, there are real limits on what can be done in laboratory. Other studies need to be done using audio and video taped recordings of normal family life. Researchers have discovered that family interaction has such habitual patterns that it proceeds fairly normally even in the presence of taping. Angry episodes need to be analyzed to understand how they develop and how they resolve themselves. Episodes in families with histories of abusive behavior can be compared with other families.

Conclusion

Extremely valuable clues may emerge from this research about how to reduce child abuse. New techniques may be developed to add to the already effective behavior modification approaches aimed at stopping violent behavior (Patterson, 1982).

Summary

Time needed:	4 to 5 years
Cost:	$50,000 to $200,000
Special problems:	finding representative families to cooperate with research

6. CHILD ABUSE MISTAKEN FOR ACCIDENTAL DEATHS

This priority calls for studies of the possibility that some child deaths listed as accidental are actually cases of child abuse homicide.

Need and Rationale

Several experts in the area of child abuse are concerned that many cases of what are reported to authorities as accidental deaths are in fact cases of fatal child abuse. They cite several conditions that may contribute to this problem. (1) In many localities, medical examinations of child deaths are conducted by persons without specific training in the assessment of child abuse. (2) In many localities, there is no automatic notification of child protection authorities so that a child's death will prompt a review of records for previous reports of child abuse to that child or that family. (3) In some areas, particularly active groups concerned about Sudden Infant Death Syndrome may have created a climate in which alternative causes are less likely to be entertained. Those concerned about the problem of fatal child abuse being mislabeled as accidental death have called for more research into this phenomenon as a way of helping physicians and coroners identify a greater proportion of the actual child homicides.

Goals and Design Considerations

Two lines of investigation are worthy of consideration. One is to implement a procedure in some jurisdiction in which child deaths receive a much more intensive review than has been conducted in the past, with particular attention to a possible child abuse etiology. If a more intensive review finds an increasing number of child abuse cases in this jurisdiction while levels of fatal child abuse do not rise in neighboring jurisdictions, then this would be indicative of the need for better and more thorough examinations in other jurisdictions.

A second line of investigation would be to conduct a nationwide evaluation with the process of child death examinations. This would involve a national sample of states and counties, and the gathering of very specific information from each: (1) Who conducts death examinations; (2) what types of investigations are required; (3) what specialized knowledge about child abuse is required; and (4) what arrangements are made for the correlation of information from child abuse registries with information on child deaths. Such a study would allow an evaluation of whether the system for the investigation of child deaths is adequate to detect fully cases of child abuse.

Conclusion

The impact of these studies could be great. Physical child abuse is a problem with potentially life-threatening consequences, a fact that is sometimes forgotten by the public and policymakers. If in fact we are underestimating or misjudging the lethality of child abuse, this could have repercussions for efforts to confront the problem.

Summary

Time needed:	2 years
Cost:	$200,000
Special problems:	finding cooperative jurisdictions

7. PUBLIC ATTITUDES
TOWARD CORPORAL PUNISHMENT

This study would consist of a national in-depth survey of attitudes and practices toward corporal punishment.

Need and Rationale

A debate continues to rage concerning the connection between corporal punishment and child abuse. Most researchers in the child abuse field believe the connection is important, although opinions vary about how. Some evidence suggests that child abusers are people with more favorable attitudes toward "strict discipline" (Moore & Straus, 1987). Many incidents of child abuse do grow out of disciplinary episodes in which parents say they used more violence than they originally intended. Sociologists argue that in a climate favorable to corporal punishment, it is hard to discourage and train parents not to be abusive (Gil, 1970; Gelles & Straus, 1975). The recognition of some of these connections has been enough to impel Sweden to outlaw corporal punishment, even for parents, as one of their major child abuse initiatives. But at the same time an extensive literature has failed with any consistency to find that spanking has negative effects on children (Parke & Slaby, 1983). More study is badly needed about the connection, if any, between physical punishment and child abuse.

Goals

One important starting point would be an intensive survey to gauge and understand parental attitudes toward corporal punishment. In the past, surveys have clearly demonstrated widespread public support for and use of spanking as a disciplinary technique. However, surveys have not been done to explore the complexity of the issue. Here are some examples of the kinds of issues that need further clarification:

(1) Just where do American parents draw the line between permissible and impermissible forms of corporal punishment, and how do these distinctions vary across social groups. In other words, how do parents themselves define abuse?
(2) What justifications do parents give for these distinctions (e.g., hitting on the buttocks is acceptable because risk of harm is less)? This should clarify what is considered "abusive" about abuse.
(3) What difference does the child's age make?
(4) Which of children's infractions are seen as meriting corporal punishment, which not, and why? Here, researchers would be able to clarify what parents see as goal of corporal punishment.
(5) How well do parents actually meet up to their ideals in terms of the use of corporal punishment?

One goal of the study would be to see under what conditions parents may give up or reduce the amount of corporal punishment they inflict. Another goal would be to establish some baselines that could be used over time to measure changes in public attitudes toward corporal punishment.

Design Considerations

The techniques for a survey of this sort are well established and straightforward. In addition to attitude questions, vignettes could be used to gauge willingness to use corporal punishment under a variety of circumstances.

Conclusion

Such a study could be the basis for formulating better social policy regarding corporal punishment.

Summary

Time needed:	2 years
Cost:	$500,000
Special problems:	none

8. IMPROVING THE CHILD ABUSE
SUBSTANTIATION PROCESS

This study would analyze the process of investigating and substantiating child abuse cases with the goal of establishing decision rules to make the process more efficient and objective.

Need and Rationale

In 1984 it was estimated that some 1.7 million reports of child abuse come into child protection authorities in the United States each year. Officials investigate these reports but are able to confirm positively the presence of abuse in only about 42% of these cases (American Humane Association, 1986). The process of sorting through, evaluating, and investigating these reports is extremely complicated and time consuming. The process and its outcomes have come under criticism concerning both its usefulness and its fairness from various sources, both locally and nationally. There are several generally acknowledged problems in the system for substantiating child abuse cases:

(1) The system in most locales is understaffed. The number of reports, and thus the load on the system, has risen so drastically in recent years that the state child protection agencies have not been able to maintain a staff adequate to investigate thoroughly all reports. A staff of a fixed size is only capable of substantiating a fixed number of allegations. So when reports have risen without any increase in staff to investigate them, the result has been simply a larger number of reports dismissed with little or no investigation.

(2) There are widely voiced concerns about the quality of these investigations. A criticism from some groups is that these investigations are unnecessarily intrusive to and stigmatizing of often innocent families. Another criticism, particularly from civil rights and poor people's advocates, is that inappropriate criteria are sometimes used; for example, that families of a certain race or class are more likely to be judged abusive under identical conditions.

(3) Finally, there is a general agreement that a poor balance exists in most child protection agencies between the task of investigating reports and the task of providing services to abused children and nonperpetrating parents. Almost all parties believe that not enough resources are available to go into the care of abused children and the treatment of the abusive families discovered in the investigation process.

The child abuse investigation process has not often been studied, in part because of its political sensitivity. Yet research on the process of investigation and substantiation could result in dramatic improvements that might mitigate many of the problems that beset the system.

Goals

The primary goal of research should be this: to establish a scientifically based set of criteria that could be systematically applied to reports of child abuse to help workers decide which cases to investigate, how best to investigate them, and when to terminate investigations. These criteria could be established by carefully monitoring and modeling the current operation of the decision-making process. Once established, such criteria could help agencies respond more efficiently to the dramatic increases in reports, help workers avoid prejudicial actions against the poor and minority groups, help reduce unnecessary intrusion in cases where no abuse occurred, and help streamline investigations to allow staff more time for service provision.

Design Considerations

The study should be organized within a child abuse reporting system that receives a large volume of reports of the sort typical for such agencies across the country. Preliminary information would be gathered on each report. Then each report, regardless of its initial plausibility, would receive a highly intensive investigation, much more intensive than most child protective agencies would ordinarily be able to do. At the end of the study period—for example, six months—reports would be classified as either substantiated, likely to be substantiated, unlikely to be substantiated, or unsubstantiated according to strict criteria.

Analysis of the data would establish:

(1) a formula that could be applied to the information available at the time of initial report. This formula would assign probabilities to a case showing its chance of ultimately being substantiated. Using this formula, an agency could establish, at the time of reporting, priorities for case investigation.

(2) a system for matching investigatory procedures with types of cases. The model derived from the research should show which procedures (medical exam, interviewing the child, etc.) were most likely to produce substantiating evidence for which type of case. Agencies could use this for determining the order of procedures to be utilized in different investigations.

(3) a formula for deciding when cases should be closed. The data could be analyzed to model how the probability of substantiation drops off over time and after various investigatory procedures. This could be used by agencies to close cases in the most efficient way.

In a final portion of the study, all cases that had not been fully substantiated by the end of the initial investigation would be followed up five years later with the objective of trying to determine from this vantage point whether abuse had actually been occurring to these children. Five years later it might be possible to ascertain whether abuse had been occurring through either (1) later substantiated reports made on these children, or (2) follow-up interviews with the children and families. (Five or more years later, children may be old enough or parents distant enough from the situation to safely acknowledge that abuse had occurred.) Earlier formulas could be revised on the basis of these follow-up findings.

Conclusion

This is a study of potentially enormous policy impact. It could dramatically alter the way in which child protective agencies investigate the thousands of reports of abuse that come to their attention each year. It could potentially save agencies millions of dollars and hours by helping them target their efforts. And it may radically increase the number of children who are correctly identified as having been abused.

Summary

Time needed: 3 to 8 years
Cost: $500,000
Special problems: finding an agency willing to participate in study

9. IMPROVING METHODOLOGIES TO DETECT CHILD ABUSE

This study would conduct a direct comparison among three different techniques for ascertaining for research or clinical purposes whether abuse is occurring in a family.

Need and Rationale

To improve knowledge about physical child abuse, we need to be able to identify the families in which it is occurring. Only in this way can we, among other things, learn why they abuse, find out what makes them stop, and determine if our broad social policies are reducing its prevalence. Currently, three different approaches are used to identify abusive families. One is the standard child welfare investigation, which make a determination of abuse based on interviews with parents, children, witnesses, and often a medical examination. A second approach uses one of two or more child abuse risk inventories (Bavolek, 1984; Milner, 1980, 1986) that have proven relatively useful in predicting individuals who abuse their children. A third approach is the Conflict Tactics Scale (CTS) (Straus et al., 1980), which identifies abuse by asking parents about various kinds of actions they may have taken to resolve conflicts with their children, including a range of violent acts.

Each of these approaches have their advantages and disadvantages. The child welfare investigation is the most thorough and is, for most intents and purposes, society's operationalization of the concept of child abuse. But the investigation is lengthy and expensive, and is performed only on families who come to the attention of the child welfare system through a reporting mechanism that clearly misses a large number of abusive families. The risk inventories are good at identifying abusers, but many individuals indicated as high risk on these inventories never become abusers (Milner, 1980, 1986). The CTS, for its part, has also been very valuable at identifying abusive families, particularly in large-scale surveys, but it probably fails to identify some of the most violent parents, who do not admit abusive acts to researchers.

Goals and Design Considerations

What is badly needed are studies that try to interrelate these different methods that have been devised to try to identify abusive families. Thus the CTS needs to be validated on a sample of abusers who have been identified through child welfare investigations. How many of these known abusers reveal their abuse using the typical CTS methodology, in which individuals are called on the telephone and in a half-hour interview asked questions about how they deal with conflicts with their children? If there are known abusers who deny committing abusive acts using the CTS methodology, then instruments should be developed that can identify some of these individuals. For example, this might be done by incorporating some of the child abuse risk inventories into the survey format. The risk inventories, because they examine attitudes but not actual behaviors, might identify abusers who would otherwise conceal abusive behavior. In any case, the child abuse risk inventories and the CTS both need to be used in community wide surveys to see how well their findings intercorrelate.

Another possibility that needs to be considered for both the CTS and the child abuse risk inventories is to give these in surveys and follow up the individuals who score as abusers with actual child welfare investigations. This would demonstrate whether people who score as abusers on the research instruments actually qualify as abusers when child welfare criteria are used. To do this validation, at least for the CTS, such a study would have to depart from the usual format of promising confidentiality to all respondents. This could be done either by simply dropping this promise (which might affect results—something that could be checked by comparing the results with previous use of the CTS), or by administering the CTS to a population that was due to receive an investigation in any case.

Conclusion

There are a multitude of possibilities. The key notion proposed, however, is a program of study to interrelate and improve methods for identifying abusive families. Any such improvements would have obvious wide ramifications for the field.

Summary

Time needed: 2 years
Cost: $200,000

10. THE ECONOMIC COSTS
OF CHILD ABUSE

This study would try to estimate the overall social and economic cost of child abuse to government, business, and individuals.

Need and Rationale

Most of the costs of child abuse are not immediately apparent to society. They involve social welfare expenditures and services over a period of years, plus the cost of problems—like mental illness, crime, educational failure, and employment difficulties—that may occur further down the line. Failure to appreciate the costs may be an important reason why society lacks the will to aggressively deal with the problem. If these costs could be reckoned, then the social advantage of preventing and treating child abuse might be much more obvious.

Given current knowledge, no analysis of the costs of child abuse could be very precise. But even being able to demonstrate the approximate magnitudes would be useful.

Goals

A study should be done that would measure the approximate cost of child abuse by developing estimates for some of these kinds of factors:

— immediate costs:
  — medical care for abused children
  — investigation and substantiation
  — counseling
  — foster care
  — court costs
— longer-term costs:
  — crime committed by abused children
  — mental health problems of abused children
  — social problems related to abuse histories

Design Considerations

The study could develop its estimates using the known rates of reported and unreported child abuse, some estimates of the number of abused children who receive services and the number who develop problems, and cost estimates for various services. Some local audits might be useful for obtaining estimated costs for various activities.

Conclusion

It should be possible to assemble rough figures for the social cost of child abuse. Not only would these estimates bolster arguments for social action to deal with child abuse, they would also be valuable for establishing priorities for action. It might be clear that certain types of intervention or prevention would have clear economic benefits over others. These would be valuable tools for social policymakers.

Summary

Time needed:	2 years
Cost:	$200,000
Special problems:	developing estimates of some outcomes of child abuse that have not been well researched

11. STATE DATA FOR EVALUATING
THE EFFECTIVENESS OF CHILD WELFARE POLICIES

This study would conduct a pilot study to establish feasibility of better state data on the operation of the child welfare system.

Need and Rationale

One of the biggest obstacles to research on child abuse is that states do not collect and publish reliable statistics on child abuse and the child welfare system. These statistics would not only be important for letting states know how their problems and policies compare to other states, but they would also provide the basis for analyzing what was working to ameliorate or exacerbate the child abuse problem. For example, suppose we wanted to know if hiring more child protective workers or establishing more treatment programs or expanding the mandatory reporting laws reduced the rate of reabuse. We could correlate data on each of these policies with the reabuse rate in each of the 50 states. We might find that a lower rate of abuse was associated with more workers in a state but not with differences in the reporting laws. Suppose we also wanted to find out if the rate of unemployment, the number of day care programs, or the number of teen pregnancies had an impact on the child abuse problem. Since states already have data on the first three factors for each state, we could easily do this study if we had the data on child abuse.

Unfortunately, states do not systematically collect and centrally publish data on most of the important facts related to child abuse and child welfare. In this respect, the child welfare system lags far behind many other governmental activities. By contrast, suppose we wanted to analyze whether teacher pay and class size and the number of special education teachers affected student performance (measured by SAT scores). All this data is available for the 50 states. Vast quantities of statistics are collected about the educational and health care systems. But there is exceedingly little information on child abuse. All that exists are the number of cases of reported child abuse (broken down by categories); this data has been collected for 10 years by the American Humane Association, but it covers only 35 of the 50 states and the long-term continuation of this effort is not assured.

Goals

It would provide an enormous boost to research on child abuse—and, in turn, to our ability to evaluate intervention efforts—if states systematically collected and centrally published some of the following:

(1) number of reported cases of child abuse broken down by type of abuse

(2) source of the reports

(3) sex and age of the victims
(4) sex, age, and relationship of the perpetrator
(5) number, education, and salary of child protection workers
(6) number of programs providing child abuse treatment broken down by types of clients served (abusers, children, etc.)
(7) number of cases of reabuse broken down by sex, age, and relationship to victim
(8) number of prosecutions for child abuse, with outcome, broken down by type of abuse
(9) number of children placed in foster care for reasons of abuse
(10) number of protection orders obtained against abusive parents
(11) number of child abuse prevention programs by type
(12) categories of individuals covered under a state's mandatory reporting law

Design Considerations

Of course, there are serious obstacles to the establishment of such a national data collection system. States would need to come up with uniform categories and systematic procedures, train their staffs, and devote substantial resources to the implementation of the system. Such a system could be inaugurated only by a concerted federal program.

However, on a smaller scale, something could be done to facilitate the creation of such a national data system: a pilot effort in one state or one region to begin to do it. A successful pilot would accomplish a number of goals. It would find solutions to some of the definitional problems that always come up in such systems. It would devise methods for gathering the data that could be transferred to other states. Finally, it would provide some estimates of the costs required to set up such a system. Having such a data collection system would be of enormous benefit to the field for a long time to come.

Summary

Cost: $300,000
Special problems: finding jurisdiction to cooperate

4

HIGH PRIORITY RESEARCH ON CHILD SEXUAL ABUSE

1. The Effectiveness of Offender Treatment
2. Therapeutic Alternatives for Sexually Abused Children
3. Undetected Molesters
4. The Long-Term Impact of and Recovery from the Trauma of Sexual Abuse
5. The Development of Sexual Interests Both Abusive and Nonabusive
6. Children at High Risk for Sexual Abuse
7. The Trustworthiness of Children's Accounts of Sexual Abuse Incidents
8. The Effectiveness of Sexual Abuse Prevention Education
9. A Study to Improve the Differential Diagnosis of Sexual Abuse Among Young Children
10. The Contribution of Pornography and Media Imagery to Sexual Abuse
11. Monitoring Historical Trends in the Prevalence of Sexual Abuse
12. Improving the Ability to Identify Adults and Adolescents with Histories of Child Sexual Abuse
13. Comparing Community Management of Sexual Abuse Cases

Public recognition of the serious scope of the problem of child sexual abuse did not occur until the late 1970s. Since then, unfortunately, there have been few resources for research. Professional efforts have been heavily preoccupied with the difficult task of simply responding to the precipitously rising tide of cases (up nationally from approximately 37,000 in 1980 to over 120,000 in 1985). Thus research on the topic of child sexual abuse lags seriously behind research on physical abuse.

The research that does exist has been recently reviewed elsewhere (Finkelhor & Associates, 1986). This literature is impressive in documenting certain features of the problem: the dynamics of abuse, its scope in the population at large, the presence of certain high-risk groups of children and some of the serious initial and long-term consequences of abuse. Big gaps, however, exist in other areas: for example, in understanding who becomes a perpetrator and the process by which this occurs.

Still, some of the most serious research needs lie in evaluating the effectiveness of intervention. Massive programs to deal with sexual abuse have been instituted throughout the country, but exceedingly few have been evaluated to see if they are meeting their objectives. Meanwhile, rancorous debates continue over a variety of policy options, and very little systematic study has been made to try to settle these matters.

1. THE EFFECTIVENESS OF OFFENDER TREATMENT

This study would follow treated child sexual abusers for a period of years after treatment to find out what works, if anything, to reduce their danger to the community.

Need and Rationale

Many of the most important public policy issues in the field of sexual abuse today hinge on the question of whether offender treatment is effective. For example, in an effort to spare children and their families the hardship of protracted criminal justice processes, treatment diversion programs have been established around the country. These programs offer offenders treatment in exchange for guilty pleas and are based in part on the assumption that children and society can be better protected by offender treatment than by traditional prosecution and prison sentences. However, this assumption has not been proven.

Another important public policy debate concerns family reunification. Many family advocates argue that the reunification of families after incestuous abuse is an appropriate, feasible, and highly desirable goal of intervention that spares children the long-term negative consequences of family dissolution. These advocates argue that offenders who have been treated are capable of being safe and positive family members. However, this contention has never been fully substantiated by research.

Offender treatment is controversial. The public and many politicians call for harsher sanctions against child molesters. At the same time, many mental health officials (and some even within the criminal justice system) argue that traditional criminal justice practices of trying and incarcerating offenders have been ineffective in protecting the public. Without treatment for their behavior, they argue, many child molesters simply resume their pattern of molesting after adjudication. They urge the adoption of treatment for both incarcerated and nonincarcerated offenders.

In spite of this enthusiasm for treatment for child sex abusers, many in the criminal justice system and the public at large are skeptical. Persons as prominent as the Assistant Attorney General Lois Herrington have stated that they are still very doubtful that child molesters can be effectively treated. Many communities have had experiences with molesters who, in spite of treatment, continued to commit crimes.

The reality is that, in spite of various claims, the effectiveness of treatment has not been clearly established. Studies have been done that demonstrate that treatment can alter attitudes, beliefs, and sexual arousal patterns (for review, see Kelly, 1982). Some treatment programs have followed offenders for a year to see what happened (Abel et al., 1983). But a convincing study showing that treatment was effective in rehabilitating offenders and protecting children from future abuse has not been done.

The situation is not improved by the fact that offender treatment specialists themselves are not of one voice. Although most are convinced that treatment is effective, they still argue bitterly among themselves about which treatments work and which do not. There is a crying need for research on this, as well.

Goals

A well-designed, large-scale evaluation study of offender treatment could have major public policy impact if:

(1) it could demonstrate convincingly that treating offenders can reduce the likelihood that they will reoffend compared to other ways of handling them, such as giving them a jail sentence. This would build public and political support for approaches based on offender treatment.

(2) it could determine which types of treatment work best and with which types of offenders. This would resolve some of the disputes among treatment approaches, and guarantee the pairing of the most effective treatment with the most responsive offenders.

(3) it could establish criteria for selecting which offenders are treatable and which are not, e.g., incestuous offenders, first-time offenders. This would protect the public against the biggest risk—reoffenses by those certified "cured"—and would also guarantee that scarce resources are not wasted.

Design Considerations

In order to be convincing, definitive, and scientifically sound, a study evaluating the treatment of child sexual abusers needs to be large scale, scrupulously impartial, well designed, and meticulously executed. In addition, it should take account of some of the following:

(1) The study needs to follow up treated offenders for a substantial period, at least 5 to 10 years. All prior research on child molesters indicates that offenders remain at risk for a very long period after release from supervision. Results from a 2- or 3-year follow-up would have some value, but a 1-year follow-up is too short and 5-year minimum would be best.

(2) The study needs to compare a variety of treatment modalities, such as behavior modification, group therapy, and insight therapy. These modalities should be implemented impartially by practitioners skilled in each technique, but they should be no more intensive or costly than called for by the standards of what a relatively well-organized treatment program is currently able to provide.

(3) The study needs a procedure for determining how treated offenders compare to an equivalent group of untreated or less intensively treated offenders. Findings that only 10% of offenders in a given treatment program recidivate are only convincing if we know that recidivism rates would have been higher for an equivalent group that did not receive that treatment.

(4) The study needs to prevent self-selection into the treatment programs. Too many studies of treatment find positive results because it is the highly motivated offenders who volunteer for and stick with treatment programs. The motivated offenders will probably have better outcomes whether they are treated or not. The treatments tested in this study should be on mixed groups of motivated and nonmotivated offenders.

(5) The study must make an extremely intensive effort to evaluate whether the offenders commit subsequent offenses or engage in deviant behavior. This means going beyond the usual follow-up technique: a search of records for subsequent arrests or convictions. It is well known that most sex offenses are not detected. This study must clearly demonstrate that treatment is not simply making offenders more effective at concealing their offenses. The intensive follow-up required here would conduct interviews with the offender himself or herself to evaluate his or her current behavior and adjustment directly. It would also conduct interviews with people in the offender's social network: family members, employers, and friends.

(6) The study needs to include victims in its assessment of offender treatment effectiveness. A factor that is not often taken into consideration in

evaluating treatment programs is whether victims are satisfied with and benefit from the outcome. Since victims of sexual abuse so often know or are related to their offenders, the results of offender treatment can have immediate and direct impact on them. Through follow-up interviews with victims and their families, the study should assess how the offender treatment has affected the victim or victims.

Conclusion

A sound scientific evaluation of offender treatment is long overdue. Many of the most important questions of public policy related to the handling of child sexual abuse await its findings.

Summary

Time needed:	4 to 10 years
Cost:	$500,000 to $1,000,000
Special problems:	finding former offenders and determining if they have reoffended

2. THERAPEUTIC ALTERNATIVES FOR SEXUALLY ABUSED CHILDREN

This study would compare the effectiveness of different kinds of treatments on different kinds of abused children.

Need and Rationale

At the current moment, sexually abused children are treated in a wide variety of ways. Some are simply seen a few times by a case worker to make sure they are not being reabused. Some get individual counseling. Some get group counseling. And some are seen together with their family members in order to rebuild trust and protection for the child.

There are a variety of philosophies that underlie the treatment of sexually abused children. Some emphasize play and drawing. Some emphasize self-defense. Some focus on removing the feelings of guilt, self-blame, and stigma. Some concentrate on repairing the bond between child and nonperpetrating parent(s). Some insist on providing children with sex education and sexual abuse prevention education to correct misperceptions about sex and prevent further victimization.

Although much therapy is being done, little is known systematically about how children recover best from the trauma of sexual assault.

Goals

Several questions are badly in need of answers:

(1) Do some treatment modalities work better than other modalities in promoting recovery?

(2) Are some treatment modalities more appropriate for some types of children depending on their sex, age, social class, or type of abuse they have suffered?

(3) Are characteristics about therapists (their sex, experience, etc.) as important as the methods they use?

(4) Is treatment indicated even for children who are showing no symptomatic behavior? Some therapists think that lack of symptoms can be a sign that children are relatively unaffected. Others worry that it means that children are denying the trauma.

(5) Is it possible to deal in advance with difficulties that may arise only in a later developmental phase? Thus, for example, some therapists feel that the impact of early sexual abuse on adolescent sexual adjustment can be treated only later when these developmental issues actually arise.

(6) Can denial be a healthy coping strategy for some children? Some therapists believe that children who are denying any impact need to be worked with until they acknowledge it. Others believe denial can be adaptive.

(7) Does therapy in itself sometimes contribute to trauma by increasing the stigma for the child and delaying the time when the child can move on to other developmental tasks? Some therapists feel that therapy is almost always better than no therapy. Others feel that too much therapy may retard recovery.

Design Considerations

The field badly needs a serious study of the process of recovery and the effects of different kinds of interventions. In gross outline, such a study needs to follow a group of children from a time shortly after their abuse is disclosed through a period of at least two years and if possible more, looking at the relationship between recovery and the kind of intervention the children get.

To be effective, such a study should try to have these features:

(1) Children with equivalent backgrounds, abuse experiences, and symptoms need to be placed in different treatment procedures (e.g., group therapy, individual therapy).

(2) The level of distress the children are experiencing prior to any intervention needs to be carefully assessed.

(3) Some children considered by the study should be children who received no or minimal treatment. Professionals will naturally not want, for ethical reasons, to actually assign children seeking treatment to a no-treatment condition. However, a variety of techniques can assure the inclusion in the study of children with little or no treatment. In most communities there are many children who because of parental choice or the operation of the system receive little treatment, so such a group should not be impossible to include.

(4) The children themselves should be queried about what they found the most helpful in recovering from the experience.

Conclusion

This study has the potential to dramatically alter the approach that mental health professionals take in working with sexually abused children. It certainly has the potential to ensure that the help they do receive will be the most efficient, the most effective, and the least likely to cause them other harm.

Summary

Time needed:	3 to 6 years
Cost:	$400,000 to $600,000
Special problems:	finding and having access to victims several years after treatment

3. UNDETECTED MOLESTERS

This study would use survey methodology in a variety of "normal" populations to identify and study the large number of sexual abusers whose behavior is not detected and reported.

Need and Rationale

Although there is extensive literature on sexual abusers (for reviews, see Finkelhor & Associates, 1986; Howells, 1981; Quinsey, 1977), most of it is seriously flawed. The sexual abusers who have been studied are almost exclusively those who have been convicted and incarcerated for their crimes. This is a small and unrepresentative sample of abusers. It is small because less than 10% of all sexual abuse is reported to police (Russell, 1986), and of that reported to the police, less than a third result in a conviction (Rogers, 1982). It is unrepresentative because it is primarily the repetitive, disorganized, disadvantaged offenders with prior criminal records who get reported and convicted. The unrepresentative nature of these samples casts doubt on many of the findings about abusers. The ineffectual, socially awkward, and emotionally underdeveloped child molester who so often appears in prison studies could simply be the kind of molester who gets caught and convicted.

The high rate of sexual abuse in the background of abusers could primarily be a characteristic of the high-frequency molester most likely to get caught. There may be a large number of very different appearing abusers who have rarely been studied.

Goals

A study is needed that examines this large hidden population of undetected sexual abusers, to find out about their behavior, their motivation, and some of the reasons why this group is not detected. Although it is not easy to study undetected molesters, it may not be as impossible as sometimes believed. At least one study has been successful at recruiting undetected abusers through advertisements and word of mouth (Abel et al., 1983). However, it should also be possible to gather information on abusers using survey methodology as well. Several other surveys have gathered information on equally sensitive types of criminal behavior. For example:

- Ageton (1983) obtained self-reports of sexually assaultive behavior from adolescent males in a national sample survey of delinquent behavior
- Malamuth (1981), Koss et al. (in press), and Kanin (1965) have obtained self-reports of sexual assaultive behavior from college males
- Straus et al. (1980; Straus & Gelles, 1986) have obtained reports of physically abusive behavior toward wives and children in a number of studies, including two national surveys

Design Considerations

We believe a large survey study of undetected child molesters (in the general population and among special groups, like college students and voluntary organizations) is feasible, but it needs to be organized in a very careful fashion. There needs to be extensive pretesting of the methodology and a comparison of various approaches. For example, careful consideration needs to be given to how to construct a questionnaire that asks for self-reports of molesting behavior. Similar consideration needs to be given to how to create conditions of confidentiality and trust that will elicit honest responses. The study also should include the following:

(1) questions that would allow a study of the rationalizations that abusers use to justify their behavior
(2) questions about background factors that would help to identify persons who might be at high risk to abuse
(3) questions about attitudes toward children, sex, and pornography that might indicate areas that could be targeted by prevention programs

Conclusion

Such a study would make a major contribution toward assessing the scope of the problem of child molestation, and also toward identifying its causes. It would also create the basis for a strategy of identifying potential abusers before they abuse and targeting prevention programs at them.

Summary

Time needed:	3 years
Cost:	$300,000
Special problems:	gaining admissions from undetected molesters

4. THE LONG-TERM IMPACT OF AND RECOVERY FROM THE TRAUMA OF SEXUAL ABUSE

This study will follow up a sample of child sexual abuse victims who are now adults to learn more about the process of recovery from the trauma of abuse.

Need and Rationale

Professionals and the public have become increasingly aware of the potential long-term effects of sexual abuse. Research contributions to this subject in the last five years have been numerous. Studies have connected sexual abuse with later histories of depression, sexual dysfunction, eating disorders, anxiety disorders, dissociative disorders, drug and alcohol abuse, delinquency, and antisocial behavior, to mention just a few (Browne & Finkelhor, 1986).

However, because of their designs, which start with the impaired individuals and look for histories of sexual abuse, these studies have a drawback: They overemphasize pathology and make impairment seem inevitable. This, in turn, has a very discouraging message for victims and their families, who believe they are doomed to lifelong suffering. Instead of hearing solely about the negative outcomes, victims, families, and professionals also need studies that demonstrate how recovery occurs. A recent survey of adults in the general community suggests that over half of all sexual abuse victims are spared the most serious psychiatric symptomatology, measurable with survey instruments—e.g., clinical depression, substance abuse, anxiety disorders, phobias, and so forth (Bagley & Ramsay, 1986). Clearly recovery is a common outcome. Research needs to document how this happens.

Goals

A study that could account for the process of recovery in sexual abuse would have a major impact on the field. Among other things, it could document:

(1) The types of subsequent life experiences that most contribute to recovery.
(2) The types of sexual abuse experience associated with better or worse prognosis, longer or shorter recovery periods.
(3) How factors such as social class, ethnicity, sex, family structure, and temperament affect recovery.
(4) How attitudes and feelings about the experience differ among those who have few long-lasting symptoms.

Such a study would give hope to many victims and families and it would guide professionals in thinking about how to treat casualties.

Design Considerations

Such a study should incorporate some of the following features:

(1) It should be based on two samples: a sample of victims whose cases were reported and a sample of unreported cases. The reported cases can be

recruited from agency or child protection files. The unreported cases should be obtained from a community survey.

(2) The study should focus on victims after they became young adults, at least 5 to 10 years after the occurrence of the abuse. Thus the reported cases should come from cases reported in the 1970s. The survey should be of young adults in their twenties and thirties.

(3) The study should obtain extensive information about current functioning, problems, and symptoms.

(4) The study should gather extensive information on factors that may have been important in the recovery process: professional helpers, important relationships, positive life experiences, attitudes that the victim took toward the abuse.

(5) The study should elicit specific opinions from victims about what they found the most helpful. Toward this end, some of the interviews should be in-depth rather than simply survey format.

Conclusion

By accounting for factors that may have aided in the recovery process, this study could markedly improve the guidance that professionals give to victims of sexual abuse.

Summary

Time needed:	2 to 3 years
Cost:	$300,000
Special problems:	finding and following up victims 5 or 10 years after their abuse

5. THE DEVELOPMENT OF SEXUAL INTERESTS, BOTH ABUSIVE AND NONABUSIVE

This study would follow a group of children at various ages to find out about the development of their sexuality.

Need and Rationale

Most of the professionals in the field of sexual abuse decry the absence of basic research on sexual behavior in general. Understanding nonabusive patterns would be of great assistance to those studying abusive ones. For example, researchers in the field of sexual abuse wish to know how adults become sexually interested in children, yet little is known about how *any* sexual interest develops. Studies of nonabusive processes will help those dealing with abuse to understand how abusiveness develops.

Goals

To elucidate the problem of sexual abuse, this study should focus on three areas of sexual development in particular. One concerns the development of sexual proclivities, including questions such as these: At what stages in the process of development do individuals formulate commitments to certain types of sexual objects and sexual characteristics as their preferred mode of sexual gratification? What factors in a person's biology, personality, and experience influence this development (e.g., hormones, family configuration, early sexual experiences, masturbation patterns)? How much malleability is there in these commitments to certain preferred objects and how much do they change throughout the life cycle?

A second topic for investigation concerns the development of moral reasoning in regard to sexual behavior. Are there stages of development in regard to notions of sexual morality? How do children acquire the ability to empathize with the sexual needs of others? How do children learn to make decisions balancing their own needs, others needs, and social values?

The third major and related area for the study of sexuality concerns the management of sexuality in family interactions. Little is known about the range and variation of practices relating to sex within families and the various consequences these have. This includes questions such as: How do various families handle nudity, child sex play, and children's sexual curiosity, and what are the consequences of various practices? How many parents experience sexual feelings towards their children? When do these feelings arise and how are they normally dealt with? How are parents' sexual feelings, attitudes, and beliefs communicated to children?

Design Considerations

The answers to questions concerning sexual proclivities require developmental studies of sexual behavior and sexual interests. Groups of children need to be followed (particularly through latency and adolescence, but hopefully even further) and studied intensively to note development of and changes in sexual feelings, ideas, and attitudes. The sensitivity and controversiality of such an undertaking explains readily why this has rarely been done. But such a study is highly feasible. Obviously, some care would need to be taken to find a group of children whose families would agree to such a study. However, many families might welcome the opportunity. There may be subcultures—in academic communities or in other countries like Sweden—where broad segments of the community would be willing to participate.

Given the absence of even rudimentary knowledge in the second area, family sexuality, what is called for at this stage is an exploratory study. Intensive interviews need to be conducted with parents and children in a wide variety of families simply to ascertain the range and variability of practices.

Conclusion

Studies such as these will create a foundation of general knowledge and a basis for development of theory that may ultimately lead to a much more satisfactory understanding of the problem of sexual abuse.

Summary

Time needed:	5 to 10 years
Cost:	$400,000
Special problems:	finding families willing to participate

6. CHILDREN AT HIGH RISK
FOR SEXUAL ABUSE

This study would follow up a group of families who had been extensively studied at an earlier time when the families were young to see what characteristics of new families might be used to predict the occurrence of abuse.

Needs and Rationale

If we could identify in advance families that are at high risk for sexual abuse, it might dramatically increase our ability to prevent it. It would provide some clear targets where programs could be directed. For example, studies have shown that poor, unmarried teenage mothers are at high risk to commit physical abuse, and this has allowed us to target child abuse prevention programs at this group with some signs of success (Olds et al., 1986; Gray et al., 1977). Studies providing similar sorts of risk markers for sexual abuse are also needed.

At present, unfortunately, little is known with scientific certainty about the families in which sexual abuse occurs. Retrospective reports from victims suggest that neither race nor social class are risk markers. Some factors that may increase vulnerability, however, are a parent who is disabled or absent or the presence of a stepparent (Finkelhor & Associates, 1986). Still these are broad factors. Studies that pin down specific configurations have not been done.

Goals

Badly needed are prospective longitudinal studies that identify and follow families to determine in which ones with which characteristics sexual abuse occurs. However, such studies can require many years to complete: In a family with new or young children, it may take 10 or 15 years for sexual abuse to occur or be reported.

Nonetheless, there is a very important short-cut alternative to such longitudinal studies that should be tried. The social science literature is full of studies that gathered intensive information on families with young children 10, 15, 20, and 25 years ago. These families and the children in these families, who were studied years ago, can be followed up at the present time to determine if sexual abuse ever occurred in the interim. Then the family characteristics at the time they were first studied can be examined to see which might have been used at the time to predict where sexual abuse would occur. Such a study would produce extremely important findings and not involve waiting for a long period.

Design Considerations

To be maximally effective, such a study would want to conduct a careful canvass of family studies in the social sciences for the previous studies most appropriate for a follow up. Some of these factors might be important in looking for such studies:

(1) The study needs a base of several hundred families. Intrafamily sexual abuse is not rare and might be expected to occur in 10% or more of the

families. But a group of 30 sexually abusive families after follow-up would be a minimum for an effective study of risk factors.

(2) The study would benefit from baseline information on the families in a number of important areas that may prove to be risk markers for sexual abuse. These include marital and sexual relations, and power dynamics between the parents; closeness and empathy between father and child and mother and child; parental absences; chronic problems such as alcohol abuse or psychiatric difficulties in parents; the presence of child abuse, emotional abuse, or wife abuse; and parent attitudes toward sexual matters and family sexual climate.

(3) The study might try to follow-up studies of special populations in which the risk of sexual abuse might be thought particularly high. Thus it might look for studies of families with an alcoholic parent, a psychiatrically hospitalized mother, a battered wife, or a deceased mother, or families that were acquiring a stepparent.

(4) The study should include at least one baseline study done long enough ago that the children would now be young adults. In a follow-up it will be possible to get a more complete inventory of the children who suffered sexual abuse by interviewing now emancipated children than by trying to look for reported cases of abuse in child protective records.

Conclusion

This study could provide some dramatic findings that would be very valuable in preventing sexual abuse from developing in certain high-risk families.

Summary

Time needed:	3 to 5 years
Cost:	$300,000
Special problems:	tracking down the families from the first study and ascertaining whether sexual abuse has occurred

7. THE TRUSTWORTHINESS OF CHILDREN'S ACCOUNTS OF SEXUAL ABUSE INCIDENTS

This study would assess whether children give accurate and trustworthy accounts of events that occur to them under stressful and emotional conditions similar to those under which sexual abuse occurs.

Need and Rationale

As many new cases of sexual abuse come to court, debate between prosecution and defense attorneys intensifies over whether children can be trusted in their accounts of sexual abuse incidents. Traditional practice in the criminal justice system has been very skeptical of children as accusers and witnesses. By contrast, in recent years some observers have given very optimistic assessments of children's capacities. The stakes are high in criminal cases of sexual abuse, so it is important that we know as much as possible about children's testimony.

Goals

Studies are needed to empirically understand and evaluate children's ability to remember and report on events under circumstances like sexual abuse, involving adult authorities, unfamiliar and emotionally charged behaviors, and stress.

Design Considerations

It would be ideal to have direct studies evaluating the veracity of children's memories of sexual abuse. However, there are rarely any independent observers of the abuse beside the child and the perpetrator against whom to check this child's testimony of the event. In the place of direct studies, analog studies—studies of children's memory in similar kinds of situations—can be done. Some pioneering work in this area is already underway, for example, using children's recollections of unusual events that occurred in their school classrooms (Goodman, 1986). However, it may be possible to create situations even more parallel to sexual abuse without actually involving sexual abuse. For example, when children go to the doctor's office, they are often subjected to unpleasant and unfamiliar procedures that involve their bodies in a highly emotionally charged atmosphere. This is not dissimilar from the kind of situation in which abuse occurs.

A study might consist of making a videotape of a stressful and unfamiliar procedure that a child undergoes in a doctor's office. Then researchers could interview the children about this experience after the lapse of different amounts of time (e.g., a week, a month, six months). The child's testimony could be compared to the actual event.

In order to evaluate some of the specific concerns raised by the criminal justice system about children's testimony, some special conditions might be introduced in the study. For example:

(1) To test the concern that children are readily led into incorrect responses by "leading questions," questions leading toward misinformation should be asked by some of the interviewers.

(2) To test the concern that children sometimes generalize an experience with one person on to a situation with another, questions should be asked about whether similar events ever took place with other people or other doctors.

(3) The question should be examined whether the veracity of the child's account was related to the degree of upset the child experienced at the time of the procedure.

(4) The study should perform the experiment with children of a variety of ages.

Conclusion

This study would give very specific evidence about the degree to which and under what circumstances children's testimony about stressful events are accurate and thus be very useful to investigators and criminal justice authorities.

Summary

Time needed: 2 years
Cost: $50,000 to $200,000
Special problems: determining the best analog situations

8. THE EFFECTIVENESS OF
SEXUAL ABUSE PREVENTION EDUCATION

This study would determine whether sexual abuse prevention education programs for school-age children actually lead to reductions in the amount of abuse, increases in the amount of reporting, and lessening of the effects of abuse.

Need and Rationale

Programs that teach children how to protect themselves from sexual abuse are being adopted in thousands of communities around the country. Large amounts of community resources are being devoted to this undertaking. Children, parents, and staff feel very positive about these programs, but there is a need for large-scale evaluations of the effectiveness of these programs. There is not yet evidence that these programs accomplish all the goals that they set out to accomplish, and particularly that they prevent sexual abuse.

Goals

Questions need answers:

(1) Do these programs reduce the likelihood of victimization?
(2) Do these programs increase the likelihood that children will report victimization?
(3) Do these programs lessen some of the effects of sexual abuse on children when it occurs?
(4) Are these programs particularly effective/ineffective with any particular groups of children according to age, socioeconomic status, family constellation, race, and family value system?
(5) Are there any unanticipated negative consequences of these programs, such as increasing fear, increasing sexual anxiety?

There are also many questions about how some programs compare to other programs and what types of curricula and presentations are the most effective. These kinds of questions will be dealt with by a host of small-scale studies already underway that will evaluate what types of programs result in the greatest learning and retention. The study proposed here would deal with *ultimate effects*—do programs prevent abuse—not simply learning and retention, and should come in the wake of these smaller studies.

Design Considerations

What is most needed is a longitudinal follow-up of students who receive intensive sexual abuse prevention education to see if it reduces victimization, increases reporting, and mitigates trauma. A large group of primary school children in different communities should be divided into classes that receive different types of sexual abuse prevention training, including some who receive little or no training. The programs chosen should be ones that have been demonstrated in prior studies to result in effective learning about child sexual abuse. The programs should be repeated yearly for a period of three years. Assessment should be made at one month post-training to make sure that those who received the training actually learned something.

These children should then be followed up over time. Follow-up should consist of two components. (1) By prior arrangement, careful record should be kept of all allegations of sexual abuse made to teachers, guidance counselors, police, or child abuse hotlines. If an allegation concerns a child in the study, project interviewers will interview that child and family. (2) Project staff should also conduct interviews with all children in the study on a yearly basis, taking care through confidentiality to discover possible abuse without exposing the child to possible intimidation or violence from family members who may be the abusers.

The information collected in the follow-up should include:

(1) any incidents of victimization or attempted victimization, both physical and sexual
(2) any reports a child made to parents, or other official concerning victimization or attempted victimization
(3) for any victimized children, information should be gathered concerning symptomatic behavior, and some of the inventories currently being used in studies of sexually abused children (Child Behavior Checklist, Achenbach & Edelbrock, 1983; Louisville Fear Survey, Miller et al., 1972).

In examining the follow-up information on these children, the key questions would concern whether children who had received intensive education were victimized less, resisted victimization better, were more likely to tell someone quickly, and were less likely to suffer guilt and other trauma. The information on physical victimization is a good comparison item because the prevention programs teach children to report such victimization as well.

This study would give crucial kinds of information about the long-term effectiveness of sexual abuse prevention, using the most important and relevant outcome measures.

Summary

Time needed:	2 to 10 years
Cost:	$500,000 to $800,000
Special problems:	identifying all children in study who have been abused

9. A STUDY TO IMPROVE THE
DIFFERENTIAL DIAGNOSIS OF
SEXUAL ABUSE AMONG YOUNG CHILDREN

This study will subject current diagnostic indicators for sexual abuse to a more rigorous investigation.

Need and Rationale

With many of the reports of sexual abuse that come to professionals, especially among very young children, it is not always certain whether the child has truly been victimized. Sometimes the child has simply been acting strangely and a parent suspects sexual abuse. Sometimes other children in that school or family have been victimized, but it is not clear if this child has also been. One of the most difficult dilemmas facing professionals who work in the field of sexual abuse is to try to distinguish a young sexually abused child from a nonsexually abused child.

Professionals in the field widely believe that certain behavior is highly diagnostic of sexual abuse: for example, if a child has sexual knowledge that seems inappropriate to his/her age; or if a child is engaging in compulsive sexual activity with other children. However, the specificity of these diagnostic criteria have never really been tested. It is possible that some or many children who have not been sexually abused also at times display this behavior.

Goals

A study is badly needed that refines, systematizes, and tests diagnostic criteria for determining if a child has been sexually abused. This study will look at diagnostic information pertaining to the children at the time of diagnosis in the light of information gathered from other sources and from a follow-up to see how reliable the criteria are.

Design Considerations

This study should be done in two phases. First, very careful diagnostic interviews need to be conducted with a large sample of children who are suspected victims of sexual abuse. The interviewers of these children should be unaware of external evidence (e.g., medical examination, perpetrator confession) about whether abuse occurred.

Then a subsample of the children should be selected whose abuse could be verified from other sources, particularly the confessions of abusers to police or therapists. The prevalence of the various diagnostic indicators need to be established in this subsample. On the basis of these criteria, a whole new sample of suspected victims, together with some presumed nonvictims, needs to be evaluated to assess the ability of the criteria to discriminate all those victims in the new sample whose abuse has been externally validated. After several repetitions of this process, the relative usefulness of various criteria should be apparent. Symptoms should be clearly delineated that at an early assessment would have allowed a positive finding on all of these cases. In a second phase of this study, all the children should be followed up to the point when they become emancipated and then questioned themselves about whether they were abused. This follow-up could be used to reevaluate the criteria, now with a measure validating the abuse in an even larger number of the initial cases.

Conclusion

If such a study could establish some reliable criteria for diagnosing sexual abuse in a high proportion of cases, it would have a dramatic impact on the field. It would greatly ease the burden on many clinicians. It would be useful in court cases. It would measurably reduce the strain that investigations impose on children.

Summary

Time needed:	2 to 3 years (with 10-year follow-up)
Cost:	$200,000
Special problems:	coordinating work with offender network

10. THE CONTRIBUTION OF PORNOGRAPHY AND MEDIA IMAGERY TO SEXUAL ABUSE

This priority proposes a series of studies to evaluate the contribution of pornography to the perpetuation of the problem of sexual abuse.

Need and Rationale

When the causes of sexual abuse are discussed, writers frequently mention child pornography and the sexualization of children in the media. Yet almost no research exists on this connection. A study in the 1970s (Goldstein, Kant, & Hartman, 1973) found that pedophiles had actually been exposed to less pornography than other groups of offenders and nonoffenders. However, this study was done on a relatively unrepresentative group of child molesters (incarcerated ones) concerning adult pornography at a time before the rapid growth in the availability of child pornography. If pornography and the sexualization of children in the media are serious factors behind the abuse of children, then this connection needs to be clearly demonstrated so that social policy can address itself to this problem.

Goals and Design Considerations

Studies of the connection between pornography (both child and other types) and child sexual abuse need to address a number of important issues.

(1) In what proportion of child molestations can pornography be ascertained as an immediate contributing factor? No one has gathered systematic information from admitted child molesters about their patterns of using pornography in connection to the offenses they commit.

(2) Do child molesters differ from other individuals in their exposure to pornography either early in life or across their lifespan? This information could be gathered by systematically interviewing child molesters and comparing them with matched groups of nonmolesters.

(3) What are the characteristics and patterns of sexual behavior among those individuals who consume child pornography, whether they abuse or not? Although a sensitive subject, studies have been conducted of those who frequent adult bookstores as well as those who receive pornography by mail. With proper protections for participants, it may be possible to determine whether consumers of these materials seem to be a group at greater risk to commit actual offenses.

(4) What is the effect of exposure to child pornography and to media that sexualizes children on all consumers of such media? A wave of laboratory studies have appeared in recent years looking at the effect of violent pornography on attitudes toward women and the proclivity to rape (Malamuth & Donnerstein, 1984). Similar studies can be done with child pornography. Subjects can be exposed to stories, pictures, and films in which adults and children are engaged in sex, and then tested to see among other things, whether empathy with child victims is decreased; whether they show greater arousal to children as sex objects; whether they report greater willingness to condone or themselves engage in sexual

activities with children. Similar studies can be conducted with media that simply portray children in a sexualized way without actually describing sexual acts.

Conclusion

Such studies of the effect of child pornography are badly needed to advance public discussion about one of the factors that is widely believed, but never clearly established, to be an important factor in the cause of sexual abuse.

Summary

Time needed:	2 years
Cost:	$300,000
Special problems:	obtaining candor about a very sensitive subject

11. MONITORING HISTORICAL TRENDS IN THE PREVALENCE OF SEXUAL ABUSE

This priority proposes that national prevalence surveys of sexual abuse be conducted every five years to look for historical trends and evaluate our efforts to reduce victimization.

Need and Rationale

If we are to attempt to reduce the prevalence of sexual abuse, it is crucial that we have some way to evaluate the effectiveness of our efforts over time. This is a difficult challenge. At the current moment, the only systematically gathered trend data on sexual abuse are the annual statistics that states collect on the number of child abuse reports. Unfortunately, these statistics do not tell us whether child abuse is increasing or decreasing over time. They tell us only how much child abuse is being reported. We need another method.

Unfortunately, social scientists have not yet been able to devise a method for measuring unreported sexual abuse near to the time it occurs. They have, however, been relatively successful at determining, after some time, prevalence rates of unreported sexual abuse by talking to adults about what happened to them during their childhood. These adults are somewhat removed in time from the actual occurrence of their abuse. Yet they seem to report reliably on their abuse experiences. It should be possible to use these methods to keep track of historical trends in sexual abuse to see if public policy and other social changes are making a difference.

Goals

To keep track of historical trends, there should be a national prevalence survey of child sexual abuse conducted every five years.

Design Considerations

The study should focus on the young adult cohorts, those age 18 to 28. It might be conducted along the lines of the national crime victimization survey or even incorporated into that study. To be of maximal usefulness, the study should include these features:

(1) a large enough sample to look for trends not just nationally but regionally.
(2) preliminary studies to pretest the best instrument for the prevalence studies (see below).
(3) questions about the sexual abuse experiences and their disclosure to see if the nature of abuse changes over time and whether a higher proportion of cases are reported and given some assistance.

Conclusion

Such a study would provide a crucial measure of whether we were making progress in national efforts to reduce the problem of sexual abuse.

Summary

Time needed: 1 year every 5 years
Cost: $250,000

12. IMPROVING THE ABILITY TO IDENTIFY ADULTS AND ADOLESCENTS WITH HISTORIES OF CHILD SEXUAL ABUSE

This priority concerns experimental studies to determine the best questions and circumstances for eliciting information from adults and adolescents about experiences of sexual abuse during childhood.

Need and Rationale

For many years knowledge about the problem of sexual abuse was hampered by skepticism among social scientists and mental health professionals that people would honestly give information about such experiences. However, studies in recent years have elicited histories of sexual abuse from large numbers of people in the general population (Russell, 1986) as well as in clinical populations (Finkelhor & Associates, 1986), clearly demonstrating the feasibility of this idea. Still questions remain about how to elicit such histories in a way that maximizes candor and accuracy. For example, there is dispute among researchers about whether people are as candid about such experiences in face-to-face interviews as they are in self-administered questionnaires. There is also controversy about whether such histories can be taken only by trained individuals particularly sensitive to the subject matter.

The question of how to improve the methodology of such history-taking has important implications for a number of clinical and scientific matters:

(1) First, clinicians acknowledge that a treatment plan for someone seeking psychological help (for example, a depressed person or a drug abuser) may be very different if this person has a history of sexual abuse. Improvements in the ability of clinicians to elicit these histories early in treatment may greatly facilitate treatment.

(2) Second, studies about the prevalence and impact of sexual abuse require an ability to identify accurately in research populations people who have such histories. A widely accepted and well-validated method for making such an identification will greatly assist research in this field.

(3) Third, child protection officials commonly interview children to ascertain reports of sexual abuse. Advances in our understanding about how to discuss these incidents with victims so as to gain disclosure will greatly improve the ability to identify and protect victimized children.

Goals

What is needed is a study to experiment with and improve techniques for eliciting histories of sexual abuse in interviews and surveys.

Design Considerations

Such a study could employ a number of features:

(1) One study should include an experimental manipulation of different types of questions to test their ability to elicit histories of sexual abuse. For example, questions using the words "sexual abuse" should be compared to those that do not. Questions that ask about specific acts should be compared to those that ask about specific categories of possible offenders.
(2) The study should include an experimental manipulation of different kinds of situations and interviewers to test their ability to elicit histories. For example, it should contrast self-administered questionnaires and interviews; telephone and in-person interviews; male interviewers and female interviewers; familiar interviewers and unfamiliar interviewers.
(3) There should be a systematic debriefing of interviewees in various situations to ask how they felt about different modes of history taking and also to ask what factors most facilitated their history giving.
(4) An attempt could be made to validate instruments by using them on individuals whose victimization could be validated from some independent source or record.

Conclusion

Such a study could be of great benefit to clinical and scientific work on sexual abuse.

Summary

Time needed: 2 to 3 years
Cost: $150,000

13. COMPARING COMMUNITY MANAGEMENT OF SEXUAL ABUSE CASES

This study would compare the effects of different types of community systems organized to respond to the problem of sexual abuse.

Need and Rationale

Dealing with sexual abuse is extremely problematic in part because responsibility for it is divided among so many community institutions.

Child protection officials, mental health professionals, rape crisis and sexual assault centers, police, prosecutors, hospitals and physicians all claim some jurisdiction. Inevitably, serious disputes have arisen over how cases should be managed, who should be involved, what services should be provided, what procedures are noxious to the child and should be avoided. For example:

— Many child advocates believe that criminal justice authorities subject child victims to harmful and unnecessary interrogations.
— Many mental health officials believe that too few children and their families receive counseling to help cope with the aftermath of sexual abuse.
— Many prosecutors believe that mental health professionals underestimate the risk that abusers pose to other children in the community.

So in many communities serious agency in-fighting hampers cooperative approaches to the problem. Many communities have tried to respond to the problem of agencies working at cross-purposes by implementing reforms and establishing integrated systems. However, there are many possible reforms and models to choose from. Policymakers have not known which works best and which might be most appropriate to their community.

Moreover, an additional problem that plagues most communities, whether well organized or poorly organized, as they are attempting to deal with the problem of sexual abuse: They have no systemwide overview of what happens to child sexual abuse cases. No one knows how many sexually abused children receive treatment, how many are reunited with offending parents, how many offenders are convicted. There is no summary data showing how many children were interviewed how many times or what percentage of offenders received treatment. This means, first of all, that various claims made by various parties (for example, that children are falling through the cracks and not receiving services) cannot be documented. It also means that there are no ways of comparing the overall systems in different communities. There is no way of knowing if highly integrated communities do better. No standards exist for what is good community management.

Goals

A study providing a comparative overview of the whole system for handling sexual abuse in a number of communities would have a major impact on the development of effective approaches. This study could make a major impact on community handling of child sexual abuse cases if:

(1) It could document in detail what happens to sexual abuse cases in several communities. This detail would include information on the CPS investigation, medical examination, all the professionals who have contact with child, family or perpetrator, all services provided, all criminal justice actions taken, and what eventually happens to the child, perpetrator, and family. This could answer many persistent controversies, for example, about how many children are repeatedly interviewed, how many children have to testify, how many offenders are reunited with families, and so forth.

(2) It could compare communities with different types of systems for handling sexual abuse cases—for example, a highly integrated system versus a loosely integrated system, a system with leadership provided by the criminal justice authorities versus a system led by child protective officials, a system that relies heavily on prosecution versus a system that prosecutes few offenders. This could give policymakers some insight into the types of system reforms that seem to be working best.

Design Considerations

If well designed, this study would take account of some of the following concerns.

(1) It would compare systems in a diverse sample of communities, perhaps a dozen in all. Communities would be chosen to represent different regions and sizes as well as different approaches to sexual abuse case management. Some model communities and some typical communities should be included.

(2) Data would be gathered to reflect such factors as:
— the efficiency of the system's operation (e.g., the time lapse between initial report and case disposition, percentage of cases substantiated)
— the sensitivity of the system to the child victim (e.g., number of interviews per child)
— the comprehensiveness of services (e.g., number of children receiving treatment)
— the effectiveness of the justice system (e.g., number of guilty pleas as a percentage of indictments)
— the long-term impact on the child (e.g., number of victims leaving community)

Conclusion

This study would provide policymakers with a crucial tool for organizing and planning community responses to child sexual abuse. It would give some guidance about the types of systems that appeared to be working best. It would give all communities some standards around which to judge their own effectiveness. It would encourage all communities to evaluate what they are doing.

Summary

Time needed:	3 years
Cost:	$500,000
Special problems:	gaining agency and community cooperation

CONCLUSION

This chapter has proposed a wide-ranging and diverse group of studies, chosen primarily because they address some serious policy dilemmas or some gaping scientific questions. They are but a handful of dozens of important issues that need to be researched, yet in themselves they could occupy a full decade until completion. In the meantime, the urgency of the need for answers seems only to increase. A growing crowd of victims and professionals impatiently awaits new initiatives from the research community that can help reduce the toll of this troubling social problem.

5

HIGH PRIORITY RESEARCH ON SPOUSE ABUSE

1. What Stops Wife Abuse
2. Help-Seeking by Victims of Wife Abuse
3. Comparing Community Approaches to the Handling of Wife Abuse
4. Evaluation of Spouse Abuse Prevention Education
5. Wife Abuse and Chemical Addiction
6. Mental Health Consequences of Wife Abuse
7. Children Who Witness Wife Abuse
8. Longitudinal Study of the Development of Male Violence
9. Battered Women in Special Populations
10. Improving Techniques for Identifying Spouse Abuse
11. Cross-National Research on Wife Abuse

The challenges of research on spouse abuse[1] are somewhat different from those in child abuse. For example, research on spouse abuse is assisted by an important fact: The victims are adults and relatively more accessible to researchers to report on the dynamics and impact of their experiences. On the other hand, research on spouse abuse is hampered by other circumstances. For example, testimony from perpetrators has been much *less* readily available than in the case of child abuse. Where physical and sexual abusers have been at least somewhat accessible through treatment programs, the reluctance of spouse abusers to seek help and the reluctance of society to incarcerate them or oblige them to get treatment has meant that there were few locations where spouse abusers were available for study. The studies that were recommended by our consultants are ones that both take into consideration some of the special circumstances of spouse abuse research and that also try to address some of its special challenges.

1. WHAT STOPS WIFE ABUSE

This study would elicit ideas directly from perpetrators and victims about what works to end abuse.

Need and Rationale

Criminologist Lee Bowker (1983) had a very imaginative and useful idea when he recruited (through ads) a group of women who believed they had "beaten wife beating," and asked them directly what had "worked." Every year there are certainly thousands of women and men who figure out how to terminate the violence. One of the best ways to develop policies for service providers is to base them on practices that have worked for those who have had some success. The idea of interviewing those who were successful at terminating violence is a line of inquiry that deserves to be expanded and refined. First, a study could include a more representative and less self-selected group of women than Bowker's study did. Second, a study might learn a great deal by interviewing men as well as women.

Goals

This study would try to identify a sample of men and women who report that they have been able to terminate violence in their relationships. They would then be asked what were the most important factors in stopping the violence, both the things they did and the things that happened to them.

Procedures

This study would best be done in a community survey methodology with a follow-up component. This would ensure a representative sample of couples in which violence had occurred. From a sample of 5,000 married (or coupled) adults, for example, over 500 could be identified for whom there had been violence in the previous year. If these 500 were reinterviewed the following year, we estimate that in at least 200 cases violence would not have recurred. These would be the couples of greatest interest to the study.

To make some determinations about why the violence did not recur, the study should utilize a number of analyses.

(1) For couples in which the violence did not recur, the abusers need to be asked what were the considerations that led them to stop, what did they see as the "costs" to their behavior. The victims need to be asked what they did that they thought was effective in bringing an end to the violence—including threats they made, services they received, and attitudes they took. All this in itself will be extremely enlightening.

(2) Couples for whom the violence did not recur also need to be compared to the couples for whom it did recur to look for difference in a number of areas. Where there is no recurrence, are the abusers or victims unusual in terms of age, education, economic security, child care situation, and family background? What differences are there in terms of economic independence of the wife, sex role rigidity, family conflict, and the severity of the previous violence? It is to be expected that the violence will be more likely to recur in relationships in which it is more severe and has gone on for a longer period of time.

(3) Where abuse does not recur, is it associated with anything different in the way that the violence was dealt with at the time it last occurred? For example, violence may be less likely to recur when wives had left subsequent to the earlier violence episode. This means that some questions must be included in the first survey about how they tried to cope with the violence when it occurred.

(4) Are there differences in terms of the kinds of events that have occurred in the intervening time. Thus the study should try to assess the effect of life events such as deaths, disabilities, sickness, separations, arrests, job promotions, and so forth, on whether the violence recurred.

As many as half the interviewees will be perpetrators, and this will afford the study a good opportunity to understand the termination of violence from their points of view. They need to be asked what the most important considerations were from their points of view in their decisions not to be violent again.

It must not be assumed that simply because the violence has not recurred that the relationship has improved or that the violence will never recur. Victims especially need to be asked whether other types of nonphysical abuse have occurred and whether they are feeling better or worse about the relationship. Both victims and perpetrators need to be asked how likely they think it is that violence would recur. If possible a third wave of the study should be done in another year to see in how many of the cases violence had recurred by that point. Then the couples in which violence had not recurred for two years can be compared to those where the cessation was more short term.

Some important ethical considerations have an impact on the design of this study. Obviously, when the study interviews a person from a violent home, a genuine effort must be made to provide assistance and protection for the person in jeopardy. This means that the study is not simply a naturalistic observation of the course of wife abuse. The researchers will have changed the situation, once they have offered assistance. However, the observation of whether interviewees stop violence with the assistance of services they receive is important in itself. And, fortunately or unfortunately, some victims will not avail themselves of services and may be effective in stopping violence nonetheless. These cases will also be of great interest.

Another ethical consideration concerns whether researchers should try to obtain information from both victim and abuser in a single family. There are enormous advantages in being able to confirm by interviewing victims, for example, an abuser's claim that he has stopped abusing and that the relationship is now good. On the other hand, these double interviews can set a victim up for intimidation and further abuse. Lengthy consideration of this issue, including pretests and consultations with service providers, needs to be given before deciding how to proceed.

Summary

Time needed:	4 years
Cost:	$800,000
Special challenge:	protecting victims and issue of double interviews

2. HELP-SEEKING BY VICTIMS
OF WIFE ABUSE

This study would try to determine why some victims of abuse seek help while others do not.

Need and Rationale

The experience of those who work with battered wives as well as the results of some research suggest that seeking help from police and shelters is effective in stopping the cycle of abuse. However, personal accounts from battered women underline how long it often takes before they seek this kind of help. Is it possible to disseminate knowledge or build public attitudes or alter or create new services that would encourage battered women to seek help earlier? To answer this question it would be very important to understand better what prompts some women to seek help at the times they do.

Goals

(1) to identify the social and personal characteristics of women who are more or less likely to seek help in the face of abuse
(2) to identify life circumstances and prior experiences, as well as the attitudes and beliefs, that may be obstacles to seeking help
(3) to identify events and situations that are likely to prompt battered women to seek help

Design Considerations

The core of this study is a comparison between battered women who have sought help from police and shelters and a group of similar battered women who have not sought help. Those who sought help can be recruited for the study shortly after their contact with police or shelter in one or several communities. The challenge for the study is to recruit a similar group of non-help-seekers. It is proposed that other battered women who have not sought help can be identified by doing some household surveying in the neighborhood of the women who did seek help. Thus, for example, the researchers might plan to screen 20 to 30 households in the immediate neighborhood of each help-seeking woman to find other battered women in similar situations.

The women who had sought help and those who had not would be asked questions in a number of areas to determine what factors might underlie the difference. These areas would include:

(1) issues around self-blame: How common do the wives think wife abuse is? Who do they hold responsible? Why do they think it happens? How much stigma do they feel?
(2) awareness of and experience with service: How much do the two groups of women know about the availability of services (police, shelters, mental health services) in their area and what experiences have they had with them? Have the women used other, less formal help sources (employers, clergy, family, friends) and was this experience helpful?
(3) opinions about various services: What are their views about the quality, sensitivity, safety, cost, helpfulness of various services, and stigma attached to utilizing them? Have some of the women had previous experiences that now deter them from seeking help again?

(4) anticipated consequences of seeking help: Are their differences in the expectation that the two groups have about what will happen if they seek help, for example, the likelihood of retaliation by the abuser; the possibility of ostracism by family, friends, and community; the likelihood of the situation improving; the likelihood that they will be abandoned or impoverished.

The study will also have to consider whether actual differences in the abuse situation are among the main reasons for different behavior. The help-seekers may differ in terms of the severity of their abuse, their economic conditions, their child care situations, their educational backgrounds, their childhood experiences with violence, their self-esteem, or the power relationships in their marriages.

In addition to these comparisons, the women who have not yet sought help need to be questioned about whether there are conditions under which they think they would seek help. These might include such conditions as a serious worsening of the abuse or specific kinds of traumas they or their children might suffer. It might include other conditions, such as better or personal knowledge about the service or the help they would receive. Consistent with ethical practice outlined in a subsequent chapter, services should clearly be offered to all the women in the study, whether they sought or did not seek help. It would be useful in this study to have regular consultation with those practitioners who conduct regular outreach to women reluctant to seek help.

Summary

Time needed:	2 years
Cost:	$500,000
Special problems:	recruiting battered women who had not sought help

3. COMPARING COMMUNITY APPROACHES TO THE HANDLING OF WIFE ABUSE

This study would compare the results of a variety of different community practices that differ in regard to police policy, prosecution, offender treatment, and shelter services.

Need and Rationale

There are many active controversies in the field concerning how communities should handle wife abuse. The early debates revolved around whether it benefits or harms a battered woman when police in a community have a policy of arresting husbands. At the current moment, debates have become more refined and complicated. Now such issues are debated as whether a battered woman should have some discretion over whether her husband is arrested or prosecuted and whether police action, to be effective, needs to be accompanied by advocacy programs for the victims. There are also questions about the utility of civil protection orders against batterers. A number of federally funded studies are in process aimed at evaluating the idea that mandatory arrest of abusers is a deterrent to future violence. New studies on these and related issues need to await some of these pending findings.

However, a variety of related issues need to be the subject of additional investigations. Field experiments, such as the ones testing the use of mandatory arrest, are not the only technique for evaluating community policies. "Natural" experiments are possible, too. In a natural experiment, rather than actually manipulating the policy, as in a field experiment, the researcher looks for situations in which different policies can be compared. Field experiments are preferable because many more conditions can be controlled. But natural experiments can often yield results much more quickly.

There are many opportunities for natural experiments in the field of wife abuse policy. Communities around the country vary dramatically in terms of their specific practices. Moreover, communities are in active flux, with new policies being implemented all the time.

Goals

This study would try to evaluate the impact of various community practices by comparing whole community systems against other community systems. Among the practices that could be examined are mandatory arrest, mandatory prosecution, treatment diversion systems, and victim advocacy programs.

Design Considerations

Given the difficulties of data collection, it is anticipated that the study could be carried out in no more than six communities. These communities should be chosen with a number of criteria in mind:

(1) They should probably all be moderate-sized communities (metropolitan areas of 50,000 to 600,000), large enough to have organized services for dealing with wife abuse yet small enough to be able to monitor as a whole.

(2) They should differ along a number of dimensions: existence of a policy of mandatory arrest of batterers; degree of aggressiveness of criminal justice system in prosecution of batterers; degree of cooperation between services for battered women and criminal justice authorities; and existence of offender treatment resources.

(3) Clear commitments to cooperate should be obtained from advocates for battered women, district attorneys, and police officials.

The researchers would need to establish in each community a confidential register tracking contacts that abusers and victims had with the various elements of the system, including police, shelters, courts, and treatment resources. This tracking device would be used in two ways. First, it would be used to develop some indices reflecting the operation of the system. Thus the researchers could calculate what proportion of women who called police ended up utilizing shelter services as well. They could also determine how many of the men convicted by the courts or referred to treatment resources ended up having subsequent police contacts. Second, the confidential registry could be used as a resource for following up victims and offenders more directly. Researchers could select a sample of perpetrators and victims from the confidential registry, search for them after a period of time, and conduct interviews with them. From these interviews it could be determined whether abuse continued or stopped—and if it stopped, why it stopped. Questions could be asked about reactions to various interventions, for example, how victims felt about the police referral, treatment at the hospital, supportiveness of the prosecutor, or the outreach by advocates. These interviews would be important in particular because they would allow victims to tell researchers how they have been affected by various procedures such as their partner being convicted or mandated to treatment. Victims could also compare the relative effectiveness and helpfulness of the various agencies with which they had contact.

Summary

Time needed:	4 years
Cost:	$3 million
Special problems:	gaining community and agency cooperation and tracking victims and offenders

4. EVALUATION OF
SPOUSE ABUSE PREVENTION EDUCATION

This study would examine the effectiveness of programs that have been designed to prevent spouse abuse by educating school children.

Need and Rationale

A variety of programs for school children have been undertaken as experiments to see if, through early education, some spouse abuse can be prevented. These programs generally have a number of related goals:

(1) to challenge and present alternatives to students' traditional conceptions of sex roles
(2) to bolster norms stressing that violence is an unacceptable response to any domestic situation
(3) to instill positive skills for dating and intimate interaction that emphasize equality and mutual respect
(4) to teach students how to respond to situations of violence, to not tolerate it, and to seek help

Although there is wide enthusiasm about the promise of these approaches, they have not been systematically evaluated to determine how effective they are and how they would best be organized.

Goals

(1) to evaluate the effectiveness of a variety of approaches to spouse abuse prevention
(2) to contrast various modes of presenting spouse abuse education materials to students

Design Considerations

A variety of spouse abuse prevention programs should be systematically presented to a large group of students aged 10 to 17, with groups of students assigned at random to receive the different offerings. In addition to different content, the programs should be varied in terms of whether they are presented by regular teachers or by outside specialists. Students from another school or another district where the programs were not being presented could be used as a control group.

As in the case of sexual abuse prevention, the impact of spouse abuse prevention programs should be evaluated in both the short and long term. In the short term, all students receiving the programs should be questioned immediately and then six months later to see whether important concepts were learned and retained. The long-term objective would be to see if the programs made some impact on the likelihood of abuse. Since much battering begins in the courtship stage during adolescence and young adulthood, it is not necessary to follow all students into later life. A study that reinterviewed students for five years after receiving the programs could partially evaluate the effectiveness of the programs by asking about incidents of violence in dating situations. If funds were available, the follow-up could be continued into adulthood to look at the marriages and more permanent arrangements of the study participants.

Summary

Time needed: 6 years (possibly 10)
Cost: $1 million
Special problems: keeping track of research participants

5. WIFE ABUSE AND CHEMICAL ADDICTION

This study would test whether treatment for chemical addiction has an impact on patterns of wife abuse.

Need and Rationale

The relationship between wife abuse and alcoholism/drug dependency is the subject of much dispute. The fact that abusers often have serious chemical addictions is well established. How and if the battering is connected to this addiction is another matter. Many professionals associated with addiction treatment programs tend to see the addictive behavior of batterers as the primary problem. If the addiction is successfully treated, they believe the abuse will stop. Advocates for battered women are skeptical. They believe that abuse often continues when addiction stops, and that even when physical abuse does not continue, other abusive and controlling behaviors supersede it. In other words, although the addiction has been treated, the abusive style of relating is left untouched.

Goals

(1) to document how much change in abusive behavior occurs in the context and wake of treatment for addiction
(2) to account for any reduction in abusive behavior in terms of the nature of the treatment and other factors related to the abuser and his relationship

Design Considerations

This would be a treatment evaluation study of battering men who are enrolled in a variety of alcohol and drug programs. The evaluation would focus especially on changes in abusive behavior toward the man's partner. A number of different treatment programs should be selected. Chemical dependency programs take a wide variety of forms, from primarily self-help efforts like Alcoholics Anonymous to hospital based in-patient detoxification programs. A minimum of six different programs should be included in the study. The participants in the study should be men from these programs who have physically abused their wives on multiple occasions. Twenty or more should be recruited from each program. Data need to be gathered about their abusive behavior prior to treatment, including information from the partners. Data also need to be gathered about the content of treatment. An issue of importance concerns how often abusive behavior is discussed in the course of treatment, and whether concepts concerning nonviolence and sex role equality are part of the process at any stage. Moreover, it will be important to establish whether the program is cognizant of situation of the wife-victims and concerned about protecting them. Then follow-up information needs to be gathered at the end of treatment and at a time at least one year after treatment. Of particular interest will be whether violent behavior has stopped and also whether other abusive and coercive behavior has changed. Testimony from the partners about the change in the quality of the relationship from their point of view is very important. They should be asked how secure they feel that these changes will be maintained. The actions they have taken on their own to end the violence should also be taken into account.

Summary

Time needed: 3 years
Cost: $500,000

6. MENTAL HEALTH CONSEQUENCES
OF WIFE ABUSE

This study would carefully document the impact of wife abuse.

Need and Rationale

The literature is full of references to the devastating impact of wife abuse, but the actual literature in this area is relatively sparse compared to related subjects, such as the effect of rape. Some studies, such as Carmen et al. (1984), have looked for histories of wife abuse among psychiatric populations. Other studies have been done on the mental health status of battered women who seek help from shelters (Gellen et al., 1984). But there need to be studies that look carefully at the mental health status of all women who have experienced battering.

Goals

(1) to examine the variety of mental health problems that are associated with a history of wife abuse victimization
(2) to try to account for what factors may affect the relative degree of mental health impairment among a group of battered wives

Design Considerations

This study could be done in the context of a very thorough community mental health epidemiological survey. The survey should consist of a random community sample of at least 1,000 women, and should include a complete mental health screening inventory with questions included about a whole spectrum of possible problems and also about the experiences respondents have had with a range of formal and informal mental health resources.

Three special kinds of questions need to be added for the purpose of this investigation.

(1) questions about the occurrence and nature of spouse abuse. These questions need to be particularly detailed in regard to the severity, frequency, duration, and nature of the abuse, as well as the time lapse since last abuse.
(2) questions probing the subjective impact of the abuse experience, as well as the respondent's assessment of what helped or hindered in coping with

it. This section would need to have large sections of unstructured in-depth interview.

(3) a set of questions tailored to assess some of the most specifically anticipated effects of wife abuse. These might include fears of men, difficulties with intimacy, violent behavior toward children, and so forth. Particular detail needs to be given to collection of information related to "post-traumatic stress"; and hostage-type reactions that are characteristic effects of battering.

Summary

Time needed: 2 years
Cost: $750,000

7. CHILDREN WHO WITNESS WIFE ABUSE

This study would look at the effect on children of witnessing the battering of their mother.

Need and Rationale

Research has clearly established that a male child who witnesses wife abuse is at a higher risk to himself become an abuser (Hotaling & Sugarman, 1986). But why is this true? It is widely explained that witnessing his father's violence teaches a boy that the behavior is a legitimate one. But other explanations are plausible as well. It may be that boys are learning something more general from their fathers' way of dealing with the world (controlling tendencies, hostility toward women, etc.) rather than violence in particular. It may be that witnessing violence creates a sense of helplessness that boys compensate for at a later time by turning to violent means of getting what they want. In any case, witnessing violence undoubtedly has other effects besides teaching violence. It may be injurious to a child's self-esteem. It may create a deep sense of insecurity.

Moreover, all wife abuse does not have the same effects on children. Many boys who witness wife abuse do not grow up to be abusers. One crucial distinction needs to be made between situations in which children are abused themselves, in addition to being witnesses, in contrast to situations in which they are only witnesses.

Girls obviously can react differently from boys (although not always), and this needs to be studied, too. To what extent does the witnessing of violence set girls up to be powerless and make them vulnerable to later victimization? How does the witnessing of abuse affect both boys' and girls' capacities for trust and intimacy? Are there "post-traumatic stress" patterns that stem simply from the observation of abuse? The impact on children may differ according to how their mother copes with the abuse. It should certainly differ if the child him- or herself is a victim, as opposed to simply being a witness. Does the experience of being at a shelter mitigate the effects of viewing abuse? Can there even be positive aspects to witnessing violence, like making a commitment to nonviolence? And, does the impact of the abuse differ depending on the child's age?

Goals

(1) to determine the variety and severity of effects when a child is a witness to wife abuse
(2) to understand what factors exacerbate or mitigate the effects of such experiences

Design Considerations

This project would study and follow up 300 children who had witnessed abuse and a comparison group of children from the same schools. To look at a wide variety of abusive experiences in the families—including both the very severe and the mild—the children in the study in the witness group should be recruited in two ways. Fifty should come from families in which the mother sought refuge in a shelter. Another 250 should come from a population of ordinary school children. These children can be identified by screening a much larger number in the school about whether they have ever witnessed their father hit their mother.

In selecting children for the study, participants should be chosen to ensure adequate variation on these dimensions: their ages at the time the abuse first occurred; the severity of the abuse in terms of the acts committed and the degree of physical injury to the mother; and whether or not their mother separated from the abuser.

All the children need to be followed up, through periodic assessments best done at school, at least until they reach 16. The assessments should cover a broad range of intellectual, social, and emotional characteristics typical of those that might be used to assess problems in any child. But these children should also be assessed with some instruments tailored to gauge some of the anticipated effects of witnessing violence, for example, how approving or accepting the children are of the use of violence in family affairs; how hostile or suspicious they are about members of the opposite sex; how confident they are that they can have a happy marriage; how much need for control they feel in relations with others.

The children who witnessed abuse need to be compared to other children who did not. However, it will be important to control for another factor besides witnessing. Children who witness violence have also generally been exposed to serious parental conflict, including a higher likelihood that their parents will divorce. We want to know what the effects of witnessing violence are above and beyond these other traumas. Thus the study needs to include at least two comparison groups: first, children who have experienced serious parental conflict but have never witnessed violence, and then children who have never experienced either. The comparison children need also to be well matched in terms of age, sex, socioeconomic status, and race. Presumably it would not be too difficult to recruit the comparison children from the same schools as the children who had witnessed violence.

Two ethical issues are important in this study. First, researchers need to be careful to protect children against retaliation. Second, researchers need to offer help for children who are witnesses to spousal violence.

Summary

Time needed: 5 to 8 years
Cost: $750,000

8. LONGITUDINAL STUDY OF
THE DEVELOPMENT OF MALE VIOLENCE

This study would follow a group of boys from their high school years to try to learn who becomes a spouse abuser and why.

Need and Rationale

The prevention of wife abuse would clearly be advanced if we had some ability to identify men who were at high risk to become abusers at an earlier point in their lives. It has often been suggested that a good place to start prevention efforts is with high school students. Such programs could be even more effective if it were known who the high risk students were.

Goals

A longitudinal study could identify high-risk men, if it began with a cohort of high school students and followed them for 10 to 15 years, through the first few years of marriage. The study should have these objectives:

(1) to identify characteristics—family background, peer relations, attitudes (for example, related to violence and sex roles), personality factors (for example, aggressiveness)—that predict later spouse abuse
(2) to trace the course of development of abusive behavior through early dating, later courtship, and in early years of marriage
(3) to identify any corrective factors that appear in some individuals to arrest the development of abusive behavior—for example, early criminal justice action, career success, or effective confrontative action by a partner or another peer

Design Considerations

The study should start with a cohort of 3,000 males ages 15 and 16. The cohort needs to be heterogeneous in regard to race and socio-economic status. Although such a cohort might well be chosen to be nationally representative, the difficulties of follow-up are greatly magnified by a wide geographic dispersion, so a single city sample would be acceptable. Based on a crude estimate that 15% of the men will be physically abusive in the first few years of marriage, we would anticipate 350 to 400 cases of abuse in the sample, taking into account some attrition in the sample over time. To augment the number of abusive men in the sample, an alternative would be to initially screen an even larger number of men—for example, 5,000—and then retain in the final follow-up sample of 3,000 an overrepresentation of men with a few characteristics, like a history of spouse abuse in their families, that would be expected to be associated with later abusive behavior.

These are other design considerations to be taken into account:

(1) The study should aim for follow-up interviews at least every three years in order to obtain relatively fresh information about life events and violent behavior.
(2) The data for the study will have to come from multiple sources. Some should come from self-reports, at least until the man marries or develops a partnership. At that point the partner should be included in the study. In some cases, however, men may refuse to allow partners to be involved. In these cases, follow-up with the men alone should continue. Other research has shown that a surprisingly large number of perpetrators will report violent and abusive behavior to researchers in self-report studies. Other sources of data should be used as well. For example, interviews with partners who had sought divorces would give an opportunity to validate some of the information gathered from the self-report interviews with the men. Another source of validation could come from the police and criminal justice records, which should be searched for records of spouse abuse and other violent behavior.
(3) The follow-up interviews would of course look for evidence of violence and abusiveness in the relationship. They should also consider power dynamics, mutuality, traditionality, and the quality of the relationship.
(4) Protecting potential victims would also be an extremely important design consideration. Services should be made available to every partner suffering from abuse, and treatment should be offered to the abusers themselves. Although provision of services would alter conditions somewhat for some members of the study group compared to what would have otherwise occurred, we think they would not fatally compromise the findings.

Summary

Time needed: 10 to 15 years
Cost: $1.5 million
Special problems: keeping track of study participants and protecting
                    potential victims

9. BATTERED WOMEN IN SPECIAL POPULATIONS

This would be a study of battered women among the physically disabled, the homeless, and the institutionalized.

Need and Rationale

There are a number of special groups of women whose experience with battering have not been clearly delineated. These include the physically disabled, the mentally retarded, the homeless, prostitutes, substance abusers, and those institutionalized in prisons, psychiatric facilities, and nursing homes. The situations of some of these women— such as the disabled—may make them particularly vulnerable to abuse. The situations of other of these women may have been a result of their battering experience; for example, committing crimes to escape from the battering.

Goals

Two central questions need to be asked in regard to these groups:

(1) In what ways are their experiences with battering unique?
(2) In what ways is their battering connected to the special status they now occupy?

Design Considerations

A distinct survey needs to be conducted of the wife abuse experiences of these special populations of women. This does not have to be done in a single study. However, for purposes of economy, we are describing them as a single study here. The main challenge posed by this study is the recruitment of subjects. For institutionalized populations (those in prisons, nursing homes, and psychiatric facilities), this is less of a problem because these institutions can be identified readily and the populations in them surveyed. Disabled women, mentally retarded, the homeless, and prostitutes are more difficult to recruit. Disabled women, the mentally retarded, and substances abusers probably can be contacted through the medical and rehabilitative services designed to serve them. Homeless women and prostitutes probably would have to be contacted through shelters for the homeless as well as through on-the-street encounters.

The kinds of questions to be asked of these women in special situations would not differ greatly from those asked in studies of other women who had possibly been battered. Interviewers would have to find out when and how they were abused, how they responded to the abuse, and what impact it had on them. However, interviewers would need to be specially sensitized to the situations and concerns of women in such situations. Moreover, special questions would need to be asked to elicit the possible connections between the battering and their special statuses. Researchers would want to work closely with advocates for the women in these groups to understand their situations and design methods that are appropriate. To analyze how the experiences of the battered women in these special groups might differ, it would be useful to include in the study a comparison group of battered women recruited from more usual sources, such as shelters or emergency rooms.

Because services are not generally tailored for women in these special circumstances, extraordinary steps will need to be taken by the study to offer some services to these women.

Summary

Time needed: 2 to 3 years
Cost: $300,000
Special problems: recruitment of participants

10. IMPROVING TECHNIQUES FOR IDENTIFYING SPOUSE ABUSE

This priority constitutes a program of research to refine and elaborate on the current research techniques for obtaining self-reports about abusive behavior.

Need and Rationale

It is crucial to have effective, reliable, and well-recognized methods for identifying the victims and perpetrators of spouse abuse. Progress in research depends on such methods; likewise public policy, which needs to know whether programs and society as a whole are making any progress. Many experts in the field have commented on the need to refine the instruments currently used to determine through self-reports whether spouse abuse has occurred. At the present moment, the most widely used instrument for measuring spouse abuse is the Conflict Tactics Scale (Straus et al., 1980). Although the Conflict Tactics Scale has opened up the door for much of the research to date, there has not been much methodological development of it or related instruments.

Meanwhile, many researchers, practitioners, and activists have been eager for measures that reflect some of the specific needs they have. And there are continual and unresolved debates about how to best go about such things.

Goals and Design Considerations

What is needed is a program of research, involving a number of small-scale studies, aimed at both improving on the CTS and exploring alternative strategies. These should be some of the goals of this program:

(1) to develop a better assessment of the seriousness of spouse abuse. In addition to an instrument for recording acts of family violence, the field needs an equally sophisticated instrument for assessing the nature of the harm inflicted. A variety of techniques need to be developed assessing this harm, in both its physical and psychological dimensions.

(2) to assess the context in which family violence occurs. There seems to be agreement among family violence researchers that the context of the violence is an important aspect that is not well captured by current methods. Capricious violence is different from violence that occurs in argument and violence that occurs in self-defense. The CTS as currently used not only does not distinguish how the violence occurred, but it also does not get information on the sequencing of violence. It lumps together violence that occurs on different occasions. Techniques need to be developed that record the context and dynamics of violent events.

(3) to develop an instrument capable of distinguishing among important theoretical types of spouse abuse. There is some question about how well the CTS, and related survey methods, function at identifying the type of seriously battered woman seen at shelters. More broadly, there is a need for an instrument useful at distinguishing among a variety of types of spouse abuse. Current instruments, such as CTS, tend to force violent relationships onto a continuum in terms of severity. If, however, there are discrete theoretically important types of spouse abuse, as some researchers have suggested—for example, situations in which the abuser is violent only toward his wife, in contrast to situations where he is violent in multiple relationships—then instruments need to be developed that make it possible to distinguish these types. Instruments also need to include measures of sexual and emotional abuse as well as physical violence.

(4) to validate self-report measures. In spite of many years of successful research, there is still a very legitimate concern among researchers that for a highly sensitive subject such as spouse abuse, self-report instruments

have low validity and reliability. More studies are needed to assess these. For example, few if any studies have been done that seed known cases of spouse abuse into a survey sample to test the effectiveness of the self-report instruments at identifying these cases. Few if any studies have been done to see whether the accounts given of violent episodes change as they are being recalled over a longer length of time. Since some of the measures of spouse abuse ask for self-reports over the whole length of a marriage, it is important to know how much distortion is injected by distant recall.

(5) to compare the validity of accounts by victims compared to accounts by perpetrators. Initial studies using the CTS suggested that self-report instruments were as valid with perpetrators as they were with victims. Nonetheless there is a belief among some researchers and activists that candid reports of violence are more problematic with perpetrators, and may become more so as the normative climate shifts to make battering less socially acceptable. Special studies need to be done to examine the validity of self-reports of spouse abuse from perpetrators, and to compare perpetrator reports with those from victims to see if there are systematic types of differences.

Summary

Time needed: 2 to 3 years
Cost: $300,000

11. CROSS-NATIONAL RESEARCH
ON WIFE ABUSE

This study would try to understand the social factors that result in some societies' having more spouse abuse than others.

Need and Rationale

Various theories have been advanced about how social factors may contribute to the existence and perpetuation of the problem of spouse abuse. Some argue that wife abuse exists because there are social norms in a society that legitimize and in some cases prescribe it. Others emphasize that it grows out of social arrangements in which women and wives have an inferior social status and thus lack power to protect themselves and get help. Wife abuse has also been tied to a social condition in which male violence is venerated. Connections have also been drawn between wife abuse and conditions of economic deprivation and inequality.

One of the better ways to test and refine some of these theories about wife abuse is by comparing different countries. Countries vary in terms of all these variables—the degree to which wife abuse is approved, the amount of gender equality that exists, and so forth. If these factors are related to wife abuse, then the amount of wife abuse should vary accordingly.

Goals

To test theories about wife abuse by examining the rates of wife abuse in countries with specific types of social characteristics.

Design Considerations

A sample of at least a dozen, but possibly as many as two dozen countries should be selected for the study. The selection should be aimed at having at least three countries representing high, medium, and low points on each of four dimensions: normative approval for wife abuse, gender equality, veneration of male violence, and general economic inequality.

To determine the prevalence of wife abuse, surveys then need to be conducted in each of the countries selected. In an ideal study, nationally representative samples would be recruited and interviewed in each country, but such an approach would be prohibitively expensive. Other types of samples can be substituted. Kumigai and Straus (1983), for example, have found that high school students reporting about their families can be used very reliably to investigate differences in families across cultures, including the prevalence wife abuse. Samples of high school students could be readily and cheaply surveyed in each of the selected countries. An effort would need to be made to ensure as much as possible the comparability of the samples, although it would be impossible, short of a random sample survey, to guarantee.

The high school students in each sample would be asked about incidents of wife abuse in their families. They would also be asked questions that related to the dimensions of interest to the study, for example, about gender equality in family decision making, or the degree to which in their family male violence was positively regarded. The study's hypotheses could be confirmed not only by a country-to-country comparison (do the countries with more gender equality have lower rates of abuse?), but also by an analysis of families within countries (do families in which there is gender equality have lower rates of abuse?).

Summary

Time needed: 4 years
Cost: $400,000
Special problems: identifying equivalent samples in various countries.

NOTE

1. It should be clarified that the terms spouse abuse and wife abuse include abuse of partners living in nonmarital cohabitation as well.

6

SPECIAL ETHICAL CONCERNS IN FAMILY VIOLENCE RESEARCH

Many ethical dilemmas commonly confront family violence researchers. For example:

Researchers need candid reports from participants about their violent behavior. So they promise them full confidentiality for their disclosures. But what if the participants reveal that they are abusing their children? Legally and morally, the researchers must report such abuse. But then, they are breaching their confidentiality. The researcher could warn them in advance that they can promise only limited confidentiality. But then, why would participants confide about their violence?

No research on family violence can avoid confronting serious ethical issues. This is in part what makes it so difficult. Certain features of the subject matter—the risk of future serious or fatal injury to victims, the presence of criminal sanctions for offenders, the stigma attaching to both victims and offenders, the intense media interest in the subject matter—all combine to make ethical issues more salient in the study of family violence than in most other scientific fields.

Researchers and funding agencies are generally aware of the ethical issues. Provisions to deal with such issues can be found in most research. Family violence studies are almost all reviewed at some point by a committee, at the university or research institute, charged with protecting research subjects. However, the depth and pervasiveness of ethical dilemmas are not always fully appreciated. There are festering disagreements in the field about what constitutes ethical practice. And as a result, studies are regularly criticized by practitioners, activists, and other researchers for possible breaches of ethics.

There is clearly a need for a systematic review of ethics in family violence research. The issues have to be defined, debated, and matched to possible solutions. Unfortunately, few papers or reports have addressed themselves systematically to this task (for one exception, see Back, 1983). Researchers can find specific studies that demonstrate solutions to particular ethical dilemmas; researchers can also resort to textbooks or treatises for a discussion of research ethics in general. But there are few places where family violence researchers can turn for help specifically addressed to the variety of situations they regularly face.

Because the ethical issues in family violence research are so important, we want to review them briefly here. These are issues anyone considering new research in the field has to confront, any new funding agency has to take into account. These issues arise automatically in almost all the studies we have outlined in this report.

Our focus here is not to provide solutions. It is rather to sensitize researchers and funding agencies to questions that inevitably arise. Some of these questions pose what might seem like insurmountable obstacles to certain kinds of research. This is not necessarily the case. They simply require caution and procedures that would not be routine in research on less sensitive subjects.

Protection from Harm

Family researchers must work under the physicians dictum "primum non nocere," above all do no harm. This is challenging because in the conditions surrounding family violence lies a great potential for further harm. The following are among the kinds of obvious harms that researchers have to guard against.

First, there is always the risk that researchers may put victims in jeopardy of more abuse. If a violent husband or father, for example, finds out that his wife or daughter has told a researcher about the abuse, he may well retaliate against her. The possibility cannot be ruled out that under such circumstances a research subject might be badly injured or even killed. Irrationally jealous and violent husbands and incestuous fathers may retaliate simply for the contact the victim had with a stranger, without knowing anything about the content of the contact. Researchers can increase risk to a subject simply by drawing attention to her. Although the annals of research do not contain many known cases in which research precipitated further violence, this is an area where a great deal of caution is warranted, because of the possible serious consequences.

A related risk is that researchers will put victims at jeopardy of stigma and ostracism. Consider a follow-up study of sexually abused children, which approaches their school to find out if academic performance has declined. If, in explaining the study, the researcher intentionally or inadvertently reveals the abuse to school personnel, it may affect the way the child is treated. It may also affect the way a child is treated, if, in the course of conducting a study on the effects of sexual abuse, a researcher conveys to parents the *expectation* that the abuse will have long-term effects. Even in studies in which classes of college students fill out anonymous questionnaires, it is possible that friends sitting nearby may catch a glimpse of personal information that may cause the student grave embarrassment. Victims of family violence are very vulnerable to stigma; researchers need to anticipate carefully any possible way they may add to that stigma.

Although it is not causing new harm, an equally important ethical problem is knowing about impending harm and failing to get help. In the course of a study, a researcher may well discover a child or wife who is being abused. This is especially tricky if the researcher learns of this through confidential information. In many cases, he or she can find ways to avoid the legal responsibility that exists in some states to report the (child) abuse. But doesn't the researchers have a moral responsibility to try to do something about the abuse? This issue is particularly acute in work with offenders, in which researchers may uncover recidivism or undetected abuse that puts someone else in jeopardy.

The responsibility to report has been strenuously debated. Some believe that researchers should operate under the same obligation as all other professionals, that there is a duty to report abuse that supersedes all other objectives. On the other hand, some researchers argue that the value of the research information being collected in some situations warrants an exemption from this responsibility, and that it would be impossible to obtain the information without it. More discussion of this issue is needed.

However, the responsibility *to help* is distinct from the issue of responsibility *to report*. Even those who claim an exemption from the need to report acknowledge that ethics do require an attempt to help those in jeopardy. This usually means referring victims and abusers to agencies, providing them with information, phone numbers, and contact persons. Providing information and referrals in a way that research participants will take seriously and make use of is a skill many researchers could improve.

When discussing the prevention of harm to subjects, it is important to acknowledge that researchers do have ethical responsibilities toward offenders as well, distasteful as they may sometimes seem. Offenders, like victims, can also be subject to retaliation and stigma—as in a prison setting, where research may inadvertently reveal to other prisoners that the subject is a child molester. Offenders' legal rights can be compromised. And offenders' legal situations can be seriously aggravated. There is unresolved controversy about the legal status of confidential information that researchers obtain during research. So, researchers need to consider that information they gather may be compelled into legal proceedings, where it can prove damaging to the research subject. Research on offenders almost always entails very difficult ethical dilemmas.

In another series of ethical concerns, researchers need to consider whether research procedures themselves may harm subjects. This is particularly important when the research procedure involves some kind of treatment or intervention. Sometimes researchers test procedures the effects of which are not entirely known—for example, the arresting and then releasing of a wife abuser. It is true that in order to know about effects, experiments have to be undertaken. But when doing such experiments, researchers have to make sure that the interventions are as low risk as possible, that informed consent is obtained, and that procedures are available for terminating the experiment if it appears as though harm is being done.

Researchers generally give consideration to the possibility that even simple interview procedures may have some harmful effects. People who have been victims, especially of family violence, may be extremely sensitive to further stress. The "ordinary risks of daily life" that are usually acceptable in research may not be so when subjects are especially sensitive. For example, just another interview—not even about the abuse—may be stressful to a sexually abused child who has already been interviewed several dozen times.

Many studies require the comparison of a group of people who have received the treatment or intervention to a group who have not. A common ethical problem that family violence research shares with much other medical and psychotherapeutic research is whether a researcher can ethically withhold treatment from any group. For example, if the researcher believes that arresting a perpetrator reduces the likelihood of future abuse, then is it ethical to have a no-arrest group? This problem is sometimes solved by using as a comparison individuals who were unavailable for treatment at the time of the experiment, or by simply delaying treatment for a time. In other studies, the problem is partly solved by comparing different kinds of treatment instead of some treatment with no treatment. In this case, however, subtle problems can sometimes persist, especially if the treatments are not of equal efficacy or if a process of random assignment prevents the researcher from matching certain individuals with the treatment that is thought to be most effective for them. Even when all treatments are thought to be equally effective or of equally unknown effect, is it ethical to continue the experiment to its conclusion when preliminary findings suggest the superiority of one of them? All these are difficult dilemmas that need to be fully confronted in all research studies.

Informed Consent

Research ethics require that participants have the opportunity to agree or refuse to cooperate, and that they be able to make this decision with full disclosure of the facts about the study. Some special circumstances arise in family violence research that complicate this principle, however. For one thing, much family violence research involves children, some of whom may not be capable of fully understanding the nature of the research. Nonetheless, researchers have generally tried to explain and gain consent from children (often termed "assent," to distinguish it formally from "consent," which can be given only by adults). They have also been required to obtain parental consent. However, another problem in family violence research is that it often involves multiple family members whose interests may be quite divergent. In research about child abuse, obtaining consent from the parent, who may be abusing the child, can put the child at risk for retaliation or may deprive the child of needed assistance. In research on wife abuse, experiments with husbands may have an impact on the wives, and vice versa. Whose consent needs to be obtained is not an easy question and needs to be carefully reviewed.

Some family violence research has ethical problems because it involves other special populations. For example, convicted and incarcerated offenders pose a problem. Among other things, researchers have come to recognize that consent conditions are different for persons in custody or deprived of ordinary freedom. Questions also arise routinely over what is meant by full disclosure. How much detail must be given, how candidly do sensitive aspects have to be portrayed, and how many rare eventualities need to be anticipated. Thus, for example, can a study of spouse abuse be introduced as a study of family conflict, or a study of rape be introduced as a study of crime victimization? Do interviewees have to be warned that they may have an adverse reaction to an interview, when such reactions are extremely uncommon?

Ethical controversies also exist concerning remuneration of subjects. Many researchers, practitioners, and activists feel that research subjects should be compensated for time, effort, and risk that may be entailed in research. However, the incentive of money, especially for low-income persons, can also be virtually coercive and distort conditions of informed consent. It is not clear at what point a fair remuneration becomes a coercive inducement.

Other research incentives can be coercive, as well. Participating in a highly regarded treatment situation or getting some needed service is sometimes made conditional on agreeing to be a research subject. If the participant wants or needs this service badly enough, then normal freedom for informed consent may be compromised. In studies of police response to battering, for example, is it truly ethical to approach women in the crisis of the moment to get consent? It certainly may appear as though police help is contingent upon their agreement to participate. Requiring women to report rape to the police in order to gain the help of a rape crisis center is a similar situation. Such coercive conditions need to be guarded against.

Ethics Toward Services and Providers

An issue that is less frequently discussed in research circles is the ethical responsibilities that researchers have toward agencies and those who provide services to victims and perpetrators of family violence. Such agencies do stand to benefit directly from research by finding out more about family violence and the impact of their own practices and policies. But research can sometimes be invasive, disruptive, and insensitive to agencies, and create grave difficulties for them. This can be particularly true in the field of family violence because agencies here are often very vulnerable—small, experimental, underfunded, staffed by volunteers, and viewed as marginal or controversial by other elements in the community. Researchers need to be careful not to harm or stigmatize these participants.

Some problems arise because, even when agencies agree to participate in research, studies often require more time and effort from them than they initially anticipate. Moreover, research protocols that appear to require only small adaptations from an agency can sometimes end up compromising the agency's ability to function in vital ways. Research studies can also create serious political problems for agencies. They can pit agencies against one another (for example, by distributing research funds inequitably), affect their image, or embroil them in controversies that detract from their ability to provide their service. It is unfortunately true that, in the wake of many collaborative research efforts, activists and practitioners feel betrayed by the process.

It would undoubtedly be of great benefit to the field if standards of ethical practice in regard to agencies and practitioners could be debated and codified in the same way as has been done in regard to research participants. Agencies would seem to be entitled to some of the same protections concerning informed consent, confidentiality, and protection against harm. For example, agencies need to be informed in advance of all conditions of research that might have adverse impact on their operation. Data concerning the agency, including such things as its identity, need to be treated as confidential. Routine promises, which are often forgotten, such as the sharing of data and findings or the giving of formal credit to practitioners, need to be more systematically honored.

An important general practice that would assist this process is for practitioners and activists to be more involved as paid consultants to research projects. Most university ethics committees, for example, do contain representatives of the general community. But in addition, research projects that have an effect on practice could benefit from advisory committees, made up of individuals from community agencies.

Choice of Subject and Utilization of Findings

One circumstance in particular adds to the ethical responsibilities falling on family violence research: It is highly visible in an arena of often serious political controversy. Family violence research does not tend to stay hidden in obscure professional journals. It often makes front page news, and is readily championed and manipulated by advocates for various points of view.

Researchers sometimes complain about this visibility because it can be a burden to research undertakings. But it is a reality that is not likely to disappear, and it imposes important responsibilities on researchers. The responsibilities concern the choice and framing of research topics as well as the interpretation and dissemination of findings.

The public interest in family violence research means that a lot of family violence is interpreted to the public and policymakers by journalists and advocates who may not fully understand social science and its limitations. Thus methods and findings are very often misinterpreted, oversimplified, overgeneralized, or given misleading implications. Thus researchers need to be very careful in a number of ways.

First, the choice of subject matter can have easily distorted or misleading implications. For example, a researcher who proposes a study of positive incest experiences will find him- or herself in the midst of a controversy that would be less likely to arise with a very similar study on the impact of incest. Researchers cannot be casual in how they frame the questions they are going to study. Second, methodology also can be misinterpreted. For example, a researcher may study the outcome of batterer treatment, and label the outcome "successful" if men show a change in attitude, such as improved self-esteem. However, if the researcher does not interview the wife for her perspective on the outcome and its impact on her safety, the findings are very weak and perhaps mistaken. However, journalists and others may not recognize these limitations on the methodology and simply report that the treatment works.

Most important, the misinterpretation of findings themselves is virtually a certainty in the climate that surrounds family violence. Thus it is incumbent on family violence researchers to anticipate ways in which findings are likely to be misinterpreted and to specifically try to frame and interpret results and to caution against other specific interpretations.

Summary

Family violence research raises an unusual number and variety of ethical issues that regularly confront researchers and funding agencies. This chapter has been a brief overview of some of the most important of these. Unfortunately, at the current moment, there are few resources to which individuals can turn for assistance in addressing them. Little effort has been made here to propose or elaborate solutions. We have simply raised the issues for the community of researchers and funding agencies with the hope that, as the field moves forward, more attention will be turned in this direction. Some of the most serious obstacles to better research on family violence lie, curiously enough, not in the realm of resources or science but in the ethical problems. Major advances in the field may well come from imaginative solutions to some of the perennial difficulties.

REFERENCES

Achenbach, T. M. and Edelbrock, C. S. (1983). *Manual for the child behavior checklist.* Burlington: University of Vermont.

Abel, G., et al. (1983, December). *Motivating sex offenders for treatment with feedback of their psychophysiologic assessment.* Paper presented at the World Congress of Behavior Therapy, Washington, DC.

Ageton, S. S. (1983). *Sexual assault among adolescents.* Lexington, MA: Lexington Books.

American Association for Protecting Children, Inc. (1986). *Highlights of official child neglect and abuse reporting 1984.* Denver, CO: American Humane Association.

Back, S. (1983). *Ethical issues in family violence research.* Paper presented at the Second National Conference for Family Violence Researchers, Durham, NH.

Bagley, C., & Ramsay, R. (1986). Disrupted childhood and vulnerability to sexual assault: Long-term sequels with implications for counselling. *Social Work and Human Sexuality, 4,* 33-48.

Bavolek, S. J. (1984). *Handbook for the adult-adolescent parenting inventory.* Schaumburg, IL: Family Development Associates, Inc.

Benedek, E. P., & Schetky, D. H. (1984, October). *Allegations of sexual abuse in child custody and visitation disputes.* Paper presented at the Annual Meeting of American Academy of Psychiatry and the Law, Nassau, Bahamas.

Bowen, G., Straus, M., Sedlak, A., Hotaling, G., & Sugarman, D. (1984). *Domestic violence surveillance system feasibility study.* Rockville, MD: Westat, Inc.

Bowker, L. (1983). *Beating wife beating.* Lexington, MA: Lexington Books.

Browne, A., & Finkelhor, D. (1986). Impact of child sexual abuse: A review of the research. *Psychological Bulletin, 99*(1), 66-77.

Burgess, R., & Conger, R. (1978). Family interaction in abusive, neglectful and normal families. *Child Development, 49,* 163-173.

Burgess, A., Groth, N., Holmstrom, L., & Sgroi, S. (1978). *Sexual assault of children and adolescents.* Lexington, MA: Lexington Books.

Carmen, E., Rieker, P. P., & Mills, T. (1984). Victims of violence and psychiatric illness. *American Journal of Psychiatry, 141,* 378-383.

Daro, D., & Cohn, A. (1984, August). *A decade of child maltreatment evaluation efforts: What we have learned.* Paper presented at the 2nd National Conference on Family Violence Research, Durham, NH.

Elmer, E. (1967). *Children in jeopardy: A study of abused minors and their families.* Pittsburgh, PA: University of Pittsburgh Press.

Elmer, E., & Gregg, G. (1967). Developmental characteristics of abused children. *Pediatrics, 40,* 596-602.

Eth, S., & Pynoos, R. (1985). *Post-traumatic stress disorder in children.* Los Angeles, CA: American Psychiatric Association.

Figley, C. (1985). *Trauma and its wake: The study and treatment of post-traumatic stress disorder.* New York: Brunner/Mazel.

Finkelhor, D., & Associates (1986). *Sourcebook on child sexual abuse.* Beverly Hills, CA: Sage Publications.

Finkelhor, D., & Baron, L. (1986). Risk factors for child sexual abuse. *Journal of Interpersonal Violence, 1*(1), 43-71.

Finkelhor, D., & Yllö, K. (1985). *License to rape: Sexual abuse of wives.* New York: Holt, Rinehart & Winston.

Garbarino, J. (1976). A preliminary study of some ecological correlates of child abuse: The impact of socioeconomic stress on mothers. *Child Development, 47*(1), 178-185.

Garbarino, J., Schellenbach, C. J., & Sebes, J. (1986). *Troubled youth, troubled families.* Hawthorne, NY: Aldine de Gruyter.

Gellen, M. I., Hoffman, R. A., Jones, M., and Jones, M. (1984). Abused and nonabused women: MMPI profile differences. *Personal and Guidance Journal 62,* 601-603.

Gelles, R. J. (1974). *The violent home: A study of physical aggression between husbands and wives.* Beverly Hills, CA: Sage Publications.

Gelles, R. J., & Pedrick Cornell, C. (1985). *Intimate violence in families.* Beverly Hills, CA: Sage Publications.

Gelles, R. J., & Straus, M. A. (1975). Family experience and public support of the death penalty. *American Journal of Orthopsychiatry, 45*(4), 596-613.

Gil, D. G. (1970). *Violence against children: Physical child abuse in the United States.* Cambridge, MA: Harvard University Press.

Goldstein, M. J., Kant, H. S., & Hartman, J. J. (1973). *Pornography and sexual deviance.* Los Angeles, CA: University of California Press.

Goodman, G. (1986, May). *Assessing the credibility of the child victim/witness.* Paper presented to the 4th National Conference on the Sexual Victimization of Children, New Orleans.

Goodwin, J., McCarthy, T., & DiVasto, P. (1981). Prior incest in mothers of abused children. *Child Abuse and Neglect, 7*(2), 163-170.

Gottman, J. M. (1979). *Marital interaction: Experimental investigations.* New York: Academic Press.

Gray, J. D., Cutler, C. A., Dean, J. G., & Kempe, C. H. (1977). Prediction and prevention of child abuse and neglect. *Child Abuse and Neglect, 1,* 45-68.

Helfer, R., & Kempe, C. (1974). *The battered child* (2nd ed.). Chicago, IL: University of Chicago Press.

Herrenkohl, E., Herrenkohl, R., & Toedter, L. (1983). Perspectives on the intergenerational transmission of abuse. In D. Finkelhor, R. Gelles, G. Hotaling, & M. Straus (Eds.), *The dark side of families: Current family violence research* (pp. 305-316). Beverly Hills, CA: Sage Publications.

Hotaling, G., & Sugarman, D. (1986). An analysis of risk markers in husband to wife violence: The current state of knowledge. *Violence and Victims, 1*(2), 101-124.

Howells, K. (1981). Adult sexual interest in children: Considerations relevant to theories of etiology. In M. Cook & K. Howells (Eds.), *Adult sexual interest in children.* New York: Academic Press.

Hunner, R. J., & Walker, Y. E. (1981). *Exploring the relationship between child abuse and delinquency.* Montclair, NJ: Allanheld, Osmun, & Company.

Kanin, E. (1965). Male sex aggression and three psychiatric hypotheses. *The Journal of Sex Research, 1,* 221-231.

Kelly, R. J. (1982). Behavioral re-orientation of pedophiliacs: Can it be done? *Clinical Psychology Review, 2,* 387-408.

Kempe, C., Silverman, F., & Steele, B. (1962). The battered child syndrome. *JAMA, 181,* 1.

Koss, M. P., Leonard, K. E., Beezley, D. A., & Oros, C. J. (in press). Nonstranger sexual aggression: A discriminant analysis of psychological dimensions. *Sex Roles.*

Kumigai, F and Straus, M.A. (1983). Conflict resolution tactics in Japan, India, and the USA. *Journal of Comparative Family Studies 14* (3), 377-387.

Lynch, M., & Roberts, J. (1982). *Consequences of child abuse.* London: Academic Press.

McCord, J. (1983). A forty year perspective on effects of child abuse and neglect. *Child Abuse and Neglect, 7*(3), 265-270.

Malamuth, N. M. (1981). Rape proclivity among males. *Journal of Social Issues, 37,* 138-157.

Malamuth, N. M., & Donnerstein, E. (1984). *Pornography and sexual aggression.* Orlando, FL: Academic Press.

Martin, D. (1976). *Battered wives.* San Francisco, CA: Glide Publications.

Martin, H., Beezley, P., Conway, E., & Kempe, C. (1974). The development of abused children. *Advances in Pediatrics, 21,* 25-73.

Martin, J. (1983). Maternal and paternal abuse of children: Theoretical and research perspectives. In D. Finkelhor, R. Gelles, G. Hotaling, & M. Straus (Eds.), *The dark side of families: Current family violence research* (pp. 293-304). Beverly Hills, CA: Sage Publications.

Meiselman, K. (1978). *Incest: A psychological study of causes and effects with treatment recommendations.* San Francisco, CA: Jossey-Bass.

Miller, L. C., Burrett, C. L., Hampe, E., & Noble, H. (1972). Factor structure of childhood fears. *Journal of Consulting and Clinical Psychology, 39,* 264-268.

Milner, J. S. (1980). *The child abuse potential inventory manual.* Webster, NC: Psytec Corporation.

Milner, J. S. (1986). *The child abuse potential inventory manual* (2nd ed.). Webster, NC: Psytec Corporation.

Milner, J., & Wimberley, R. (1980). An inventory for the identification of child abusers. *Journal of Clinical Psychology, 35,* 95-100.

Moore, D., & Straus, M. (1987). *Survey of physical child abuse in New Hampshire.* Durham, NH: Family Research Laboratory.

Olds, D., Henderson, C. R., Chamberlin, R., & Tatelbaum, R. (1986). The prevention of child abuse and neglect: A randomized trial of nurse home visitation. *Pediatrics 78* (1), 65-78.

Pagelow, M. D. (1981). *Women-Battering: Victims and Their Experiences.* Beverly Hills, CA: Sage Publications.

Parke, R. D., & Slaby, R. G. (1983). The development of aggression. In P. H. Mussen (Ed.), *Handbook of child psychology (Vol. 10)* (pp. 547-641). New York: John Wiley.

Patterson, G. R. (1982). *Coercive family process.* Eugene, OR: Castalia.

Pillemer, K., & Finkelhor, D. (1988). The prevalence of elder abuse: A random sample survey. *The Gerontologist 28*(1), 51-57.

Quinsey, V. L. (1977). The assessment and treatment of child molesters: A review. *Canadian Psychological Review, 18*(3), 204-220.

Reid, J. (1986). Social interaction patterns in families of abused and non-abused children. In C. Zahn-Wexler, M. Cummings, & R. Iannotti (Eds.), *Altruism and aggression.* Cambridge, MA: Cambridge Press.

Rogers, C. (1982). Child sexual abuse and the courts: Preliminary findings. In J. R. Conte & D. Shore (Eds.), *Social work and child sexual abuse.* New York: Haworth.

Russell, D. (1982). *Rape in marriage.* New York: Macmillan.

Russell, D. (1983). The incidence and prevalence of intrafamilial and extrafamilial sexual abuse of female children. *Child Abuse and Neglect, 7,* 133-146.

Russell, D. (1986). *The secret trauma: Incest in the lives of girls and women.* New York: Basic Books.

Sherman, L., & Berk, R. (1984). The specific deterrent effects of arrest for domestic assault. *American Sociological Review, 49,* 261-272.

Siegel, J., Burnam, M., Stein, J., Goldberg, T., & Sorenson, S. (1986). *Sexual assault and psychiatric disorder.* Report submitted to National Institute of Mental Health.

Smith, S. (1984). Significant research findings in the etiology of child abuse. *Social Casework, 65,* (6), 337-346.

Starr, R. H., Jr. (1982). *Child abuse prediction: Policy implications.* Cambridge, MA: Ballinger.

Steinmetz, S.K.,&Straus, M.A. (1974).*Violence in the Family.*New York:Harper and Row.

Straus, M. A., & Gelles, R. (1986). Societal change and change in family violence from 1975 to 1985 as revealed by two national surveys. *Journal of Marriage and the Family, 48,* 465-479.

Straus, M. A., Gelles, R., & Steinmetz, S. (1980). *Behind closed doors: Violence in the American family.* Garden City, NY: Doubleday.

Timnick, L. (1985a). 22% in survey were child abuse victims. *Los Angeles Times,* p. 1, August 25.

Tufts' New England Medical Center, Division of Child Psychiatry (1984). Sexually exploited children: Service and research project (Final report for the Office of Juvenile Justice and Delinquency Prevention). Washington, DC: Department of Justice.

Wolfe, D. (1985). Child abusive parents: An empirical review and analysis. *Psychological Bulletin, 97,* 462-482.

ABOUT THE AUTHORS

David Finkelhor is the Associate Director of the Family Research Laboratory and the Family Violence Research Program at the University of New Hampshire. His latest publication is *Sourcebook on Child Sexual Abuse* (Sage, 1986), a compilation of research on the subject of sexual abuse. He has been studying the problem of family violence since 1977, and has published two other books, *License to Rape* (Free Press), and *Child Sexual Abuse: New Theory and Research* (Free Press), and over two dozen articles on the subject. He is coeditor of *The Dark Side of Families* (Sage) and the recipient of grants from the National Institute of Mental Health, and the National Center on Child Abuse and Neglect.

Gerald T. Hotaling is Assistant Professor in the Department of Criminal Justice at the University of Lowell and Research Associate of the Family Research Laboratory at the University of New Hampshire. He has edited two books on family violence and has been the recipient of a number of grants on violence and child sexual abuse.

Kersti Yllö is currently Associate Professor of Sociology and Coordinator of the Gender-Balanced Curriculum Project at Wheaton College in Norton, MA. She received her Ph.D. in Sociology from the University of New Hampshire, where she also held a postdoctoral fellowship at the Family Violence Research Program. She has published articles on cohabitation, the status of women, and wife abuse, and is coauthor, with D. Finkelhor, of *License to Rape: Sexual Abuse of Wives* (Free Press).